Visual Basi

Visual Basic ® 6 Made Easy

A Complete Tutorial for Beginners

Liew Voon Kiong

Disclaimer

Visual Basic® Made Easy- A Complete Tutorial for Beginners is an independent publication and is not affiliated with, nor has it been authorized, sponsored, or otherwise approved by Microsoft Corporation.

Trademarks

Microsoft, Visual Basic, Excel, Acess and Windows are either registered trademarks or trademarks of Microsoft Corporation in the United States and/or other countries. All other trademarks belong to their respective owners.

Liability

The purpose of this book is to provide a basic guide for people interested in Visual Basic® programming. Although every effort and care has been taken to make the information as accurate as possible, the author shall not be liable for any error, harm or damage arising from using the instructions given in this book.

ISBN : 1-4196-2895-X

To order additional copies, please contact us.
BookSurge, LLC
www.booksurge.com
1-866-308-6235
orders@booksurge.com

Visual Basic ® 6 Made Easy

CONTENTS

Acknowledgement

I would like to express my sincere gratitude to many people who have made their contributions in one way or another to the successful publication of this book.

My special thanks go to my children Xiang, Yi and Xun. My daughter Xiang edited this book while my sons Yi and Xun contributed their ideas and even wrote some of the sample programs for this book. I would also like to appreciate the support provided by my beloved wife Kim Huang and my youngest daughter Yuan. Besdies, I would like to thank the million of visitors to my Visual Basic ® Tutorial website at www.vbtutor.net, especially those who contributed their comments, for their support and encouragement. Finally, I would like to thank my publisher BookSurge for the guidance and assistance in producing this book.

About the Author

D r. Liew Voon Kiong holds a bachelor degree in Mathematics, a master degree in Management and a doctoral degree in Business Administration. He has been involved in programming for more than 15 years. He created the popular online Visual Basic® Tutorial at www.vbtutor.net in 1996 and since then the web site has attracted millions of visitors and it is one of the top searched Visual Basic® Tutorial websites in many search engines including Google. In order to provide more support for the Visual Basic® hobbyists, he has written this book based on the Visual Basic® tutorial.

Lesson 1

Introduction to Visual Basic®

- A brief description of Visual Basic
- Getting to know the Visual Basic environment

1.1 A brief description of Visual Basic

VISUAL BASIC® is a high level programming language evolved from the earlier DOS version called BASIC. BASIC stands for Beginners' All-purpose Symbolic Instruction Code. The program codes in Visual Basic ® resemble the English language. Different software companies produce different versions of BASIC, such as Microsoft ® QBASIC, QUICKBASIC, GWBASIC, and IBM BASICA.

Visual Basic is a fairly easy programming language and it is for anybody who is interested in programming but lacks professional training in software engineering. Learning Visual Basic will help young children to improve their logical thinking skills and develop their minds. You can choose to program in Visual Basic purely for fun and enjoyment or create more advanced applications such as educational courseware and commercial software.

Visual Basic is a visual and events driven Programming Language. These are the main divergences from the old BASIC. In BASIC, programming is done in a text-based environment and the program is executed sequentially. In Visual Basic, programming is done in a graphical environment. In old BASIC, you have to write a text-based procedure to design the interface, but Visual Basic enables you to design the interface by dragging and resizing the objects as well as changing their colors, just like any Windows®-based programs.

Visual Basic is event-driven because users may click on a certain object randomly, so each object has to be programmed independently to be able to respond to those actions (events). Examples of events are clicking a command button, entering text into a text box, selecting an item in a list box etc. Therefore, a Visual Basic program is made up of many subprograms; each with its own program code, which can be executed independently and at the same time can be linked together in one way or another.

1.2 The Visual Basic Environment

Upon start up, Visual Basic 6 will display the dialog box as shown in Figure 1.1. You can choose to start a new project, open an existing project or select a list of recently opened programs. A project is a collection of files that make up your application. There are various types of applications that can be created; however, we shall concentrate on creating Standard EXE programs (EXE means executable). Now, click on the Standard EXE icon to go into the Visual Basic programming environment.

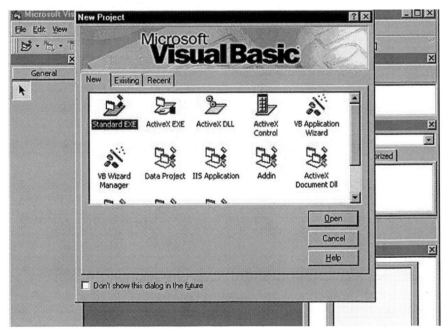

Figure 1.1 The Visual Basic Start-up Dialog Box

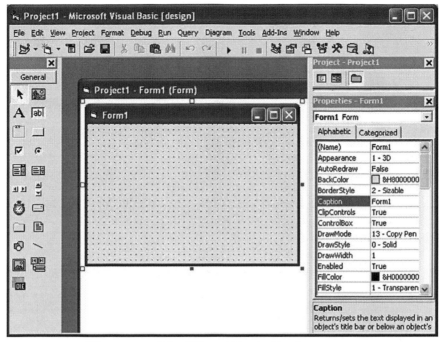

Figure 1.2: The Visual Basic Environment

As shown in Figure 1.2, the Visual Basic Environment consists of
- A blank form for you to design your application's interface.
- The project window which displays the files that are created in your application.
- The properties window which displays the properties of various controls and objects that are created in your application.

It also has a Toolbox that consists of all the controls essential for developing a Visual Basic Application. The controls include text boxes, command buttons, labels, combo boxes, picture boxes, image boxes, timers and other objects that can be dragged and drawn on the form to perform certain tasks according to the events assigned to them. You may also add additional objects. First, click on the project item on the menu, then on the components item on the drop-down list, and lastly select the controls you want to use in your program. The controls for Standard.EXE window are shown in Figure 1.3.

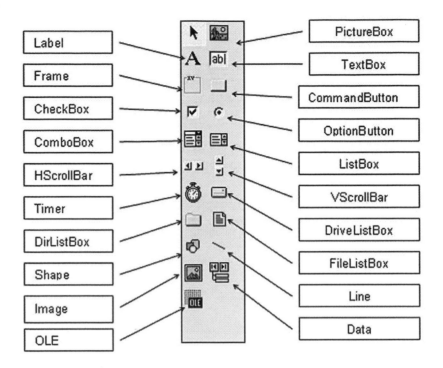

Figure 1.3: The controls available for a Standard.exe project

Exercise 1

1. Write down the meaning of BASIC.
2. Briefly explain the difference between VISUAL BASIC and the old BASIC.
3. List out all the controls in a Standard.exe Visual Basic project.

Lesson 2

Building the Visual Basic Applications

- Creating simple Visual Basic Applications.
- Getting to know the steps in building a Visual Basic Application.

2.1 Creating Simple Visual Basic Applications

In this section, we are not going into the technical aspects of Visual Basic programming. The main purpose of this section is to let you get a feel for it by trying out a few examples in this lesson. Example 2.1 is a simple program. First of all, you have to launch Microsoft Visual Basic. Normally, a default form Form1 will be available for you to start your new project. Double click on Form1, and the source code window as shown in Figure 2.1 will appear. The top of the source code window consists of a list of objects (on the left) and their associated events or procedures (on the right). In Figure 2.1, the object displayed is Form and the associated procedure is Load.

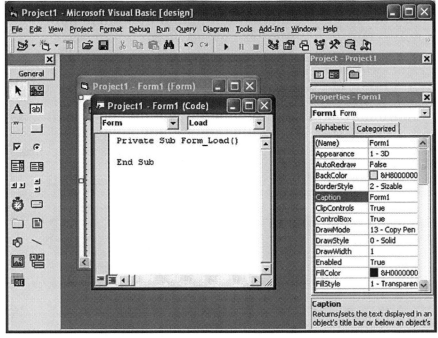

Figure 2.1 The Source Code Window

When you click on the object box, the drop-down list will display a list of objects you have inserted into your form as shown in Figure 2.2. Here, you can see the form, the command button with the name Command1, the label with the name Label1 and the PictureBox with the name Picture1. Similarly, when you click on the procedure box, a list of procedures associated with the object will be displayed as shown in Figure 2.3. Some of the procedures associated with the object Form are Activate, Click, DblClick (Double-Click), DragDrop, keyPress etc. Each object has its own set of procedures. You can select an object and write codes for any of its procedures in order to perform certain tasks.

Figure 2.2: List of Objects

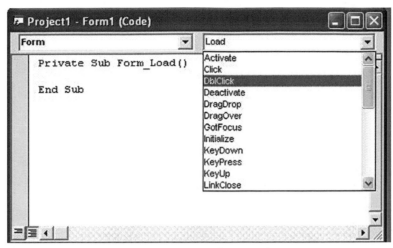

Figure 2.3: List of Procedures

You don't have to worry about the beginning and end statements (i.e. Private Sub Form_Load.......End Sub), just key in the codes between the above two statements exactly as shown here. When you run the program, don't be surprised that nothing shows up. In order to display the output of the program, you have to add the Form1.show statement like in Example 2.1 or you can just use the Form_Activate ( ) event procedure as shown in example 2.2. The command Print does not mean printing using a printer. Instead, it means displaying the output on the computer screen. Now, press F5 or click on the run button to run the program and you will get the output as shown in Figure 2.4.

Example 2.1
Private Sub Form_Load ( )
Form1.show
Print "Welcome to Visual Basic tutorial"
End Sub

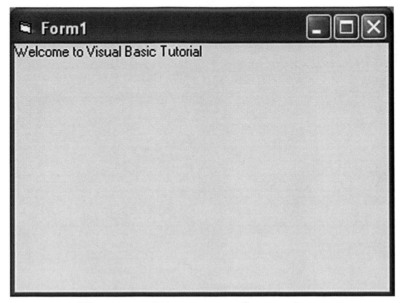

Figure 2.4 : The output of example 2.1.

You can also perform simple arithmetic calculations as shown in example 2.2. Visual Basic uses * to denote the multiplication operator and / to denote the division operator. The output is shown in Figure 2.5, where the results are arranged vertically.

Example 2.2
```
Private Sub Form_Activate ( )
Print 20 + 10
Print 20 — 10
Print 20 * 10
Print 20 / 10
End Sub
```

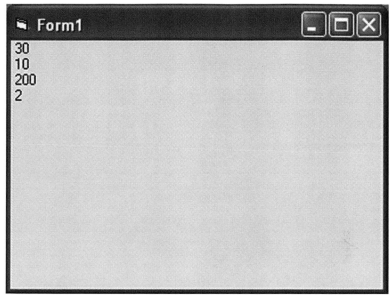

Figure 2.5: The output of example 2.2

Example 2.2 can also be written as
Private Sub Form_Activate ( )
Print 20 + 10, 20 — 10, 20 * 10, 20 / 10
End Sub

The numbers will be arranged in a horizontal line separated by spaces as shown in Figure 2.6:

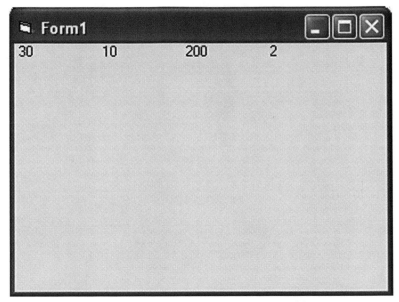

Figure 2.6: Output in a horizontal line

Example 2.3 is an improved version of example 2.2 as it employs two variables, x and y, and assigns initial values of 20 and 10 to them respectively. When you need to change the values of x and y, just change the initial values instead of every individual value which is more time consuming.

Example 2.3
```
Private Sub Form_Activate ( )
x = 20
y = 10
Print x + y
Print x—y
Print x * y
Print x / y
End Sub
```

You can also use the + or the & operator to join two or more texts (string) together like in example 2. 4 (a) and (b)

Example 2.4(a)
```
Private Sub Form_Activate ()
```

A = "Tom"
B= "likes"
C= "to"
D = "eat"
E = "burgers."
Print A + B + C + D + E
End Sub

Example 2. 4(b)
Private Sub Form_Activate ()
A = "Tom"
B= "likes"
C= "to"
D = "eat"
E = "burgers."
Print A & B & C & D & E
End Sub

The output is shown in Figure 2.7

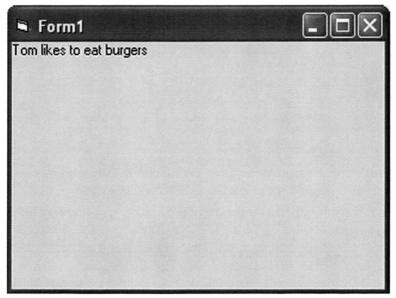

Figure 2.7: The Output of Example 2.4(a) &(b)

2.2 Steps in Building a Visual Basic Application

Generally, there are three basic steps in building a Visual Basic application. The steps are as follows:

Step 1: Design the interface.

Step 2: Set the properties of the controls.

Step 3: Write the events' procedures.

Example 2.5

This program is a simple program which calculates the volume of a cylinder.

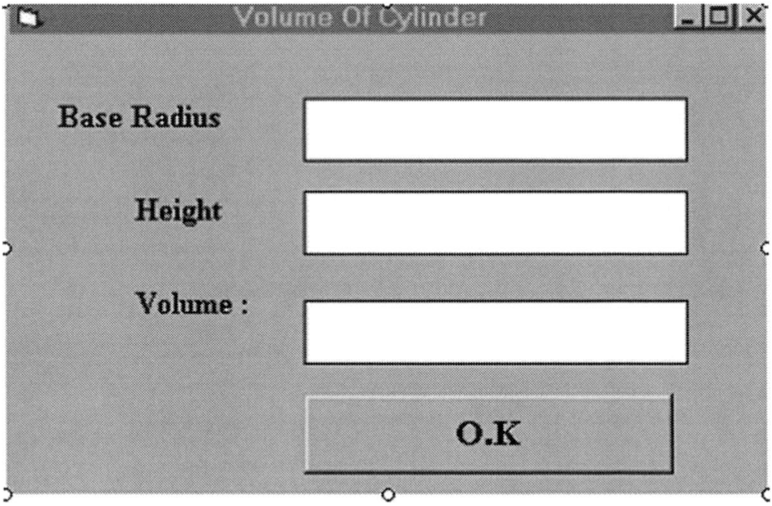

Figure 2.8 A Program to Calculate the Volume of a Cylinder

First of all, go to the properties window and change the form caption to Volume of Cylinder, then drag and insert three labels into the form and change their captions to Base Radius, Height and Volume respectively. After that, insert three text boxes and clear the text contents so that you get three empty boxes. Name the text boxes as radius, hght and volume respectively. Lastly, insert a command button and change its caption to O.K and its name to OK. Now save the project as cylinder.vbp and the form as cylinder.frm. For now we shall leave out the codes which you will learn in the following lessons.

Example 2.6

Designing an attractive and user friendly interface is the first step in building a Visual Basic program. To illustrate this point, let's look at the calculator program.

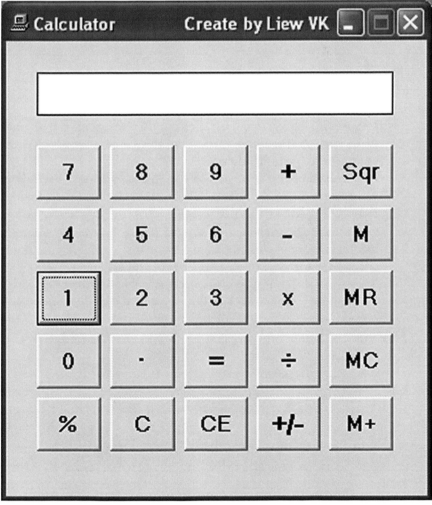

Figure 2.9 Calculator

Follow the steps below to design the calculator interface:
- Resize the form until you get the size you are satisfied with.
- Go to the properties window and change the default caption of the form to the caption you like, such as Calculator.
- Change the other properties of the form, such as background color, foreground color, and border style. For this particular program, I recommend you set the following properties for Form1:

BorderStyle Fixed Single
MaxButton   False
minButton   True

These properties will ensure that the users cannot resize or maximize your calculator window, but will be able to minimize the window.
- Draw the Display Panel by clicking on the Label button and place your mouse on the form. Start drawing by pressing down your mouse button and dragging it.
- Click on the panel and the corresponding properties window will appear. Clear the default label so that the caption is blank. It is better to set the background color to a brighter color while the foreground color should be of a darker color like black (for easy viewing). Change the name to 'display' as I am going to use it later to write codes for the calculator.
- Now draw the command buttons that are necessary to operate a calculator. I suggest you follow exactly what is shown in the image above.

Now run the project by pressing F5. If you are satisfied with the appearance, go ahead and save the project.

Exercise 2
1. Write down the list of procedures which are associated with the Form object.
2. Write a program to display the sentence "I like Visual Basic".
3. Write a program to compute the value of 1500+1000-450x10+300÷5.
4. Assigning a value of 9 to x and a value of 13 to y, and write a program to compute the values of 2x+y, (x+y)÷2 and x^2y.

Lesson 3

Managing the Controls

- Setting the properties of the controls
- Learning how to work with the controls

3.1 The Properties of the Controls

Before writing an event procedure for the control to respond to a user's input, you have to set certain properties for the control to determine its appearance and how it will work with the event procedure. You can set the properties of the controls in the properties window at design phase or at runtime.

Figure 3.1 is a typical properties window for a form. You can rename the form caption to any name you like. In the properties window, the item which appears at the top part is the object currently selected (in Figure 3.1, the object selected is Form1). At the bottom part, the items listed in the left column represent the names of various properties associated with the selected object while the items listed in the right column represent the states of the properties. Properties can be set by highlighting the items in the right column and then changing them by typing or selecting the options available. For example, in order to change the caption, just highlight Form1 under the name Caption and change it to another name. You may also alter the appearance of the form by setting it to 3D or flat. And you can do other things like changing the foreground and background color, changing the font type and font size, enabling or disabling the minimize and maximize buttons etc.

You can also change the properties at runtime to produce special effects such as changing of colors, shapes, animation effects and so on. For example the following code will change the form color to red every time the form is loaded. Visual Basic uses the hexadecimal system to represent colors. You can check the color codes in the properties windows which are shown under ForeColor and BackColor .

```
Private Sub Form_Load()
Form1.Show
Form1.BackColor = &H000000FF&
End Sub
```

Figure 3.1

Another example is to change the control Shape to a particular shape at runtime by writing the following code. This code will change the shape to a circle at runtime. Later you will learn how to change the shapes randomly by using the RND function.

```
Private Sub Form_Load()
Shape1.Shape = 3
```

End Sub

I would like to stress that learning how and when to set the objects' properties is very important as it can help you to write a good program. So, I advise you to spend a lot of time playing with the objects' properties. I am not going into the details on how to set the properties, however, I would like to stress a few important points:

- You should set the Caption Property of a control clearly so that the user knows what to do with that command. For example, in the calculator program, as all the captions of the command buttons such as +, −, MC, MR are commonly found in an ordinary calculator, the user should have no problems in manipulating the buttons.

- A lot of programmers like to use a meaningful name for the Name Property because it is easier for them to write and read the event procedure and easier to debug or modify the programs later. However, it is not a must to do that as long as you label your objects clearly and use comments in the program whenever you feel necessary.

- One more important property is whether the control is being enabled or not.

- Finally, you must also consider making the control visible or invisible at runtime, or when should it become visible or invisible.

3.2 Handling some of the common controls

a) The Text Box

The text box is the standard control that is used to receive input from the user as well as to display the output. It can handle string (text) and numeric data but not images or pictures. Strings in a text box can be converted to numeric data by using the function Val(text). The following example illustrates a simple program that processes input from the user.

Example 3.1

In this program, two text boxes are inserted into the form together with a few labels. The two text boxes are used to accept input from the user and one of the labels will be used to display the sum of two numbers that are entered into the two text boxes. A command button is also programmed to calculate the sum of the two numbers using the plus operator. The program creates a variable, 'sum', to accept the summation of values from the Text1 textbox and the Text2 textbox. The procedure to calculate and display the output on the label is shown below. The output is shown in Figure 3.2.

```
Private Sub Command1_Click()
'To add the values in the Text1 textbox and the Text2 textbox
Sum = Val(Text1.Text) + Val(Text2.Text)
'To display the answer on label 1
Label1.Caption = Sum
End Sub
```

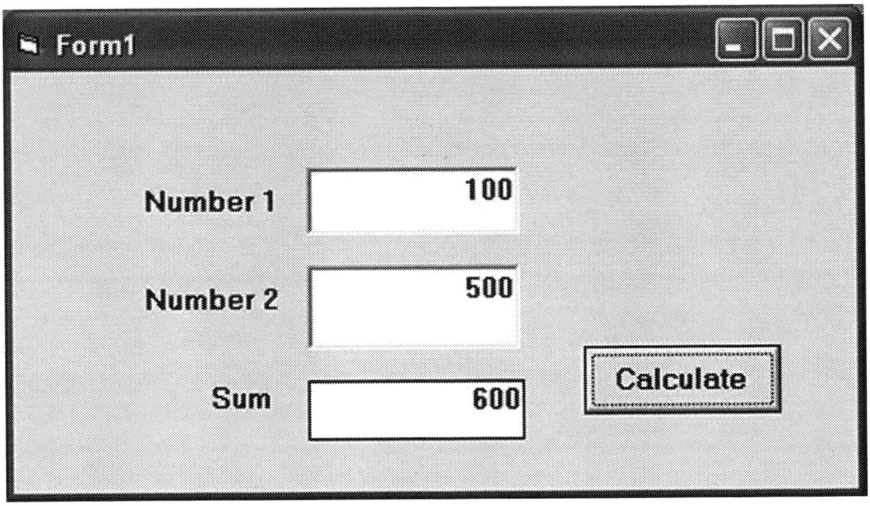

Figure 3.2

b) The Label

The label is a very useful control for Visual Basic, as it is not only used to provide instructions and guides for the users, it can also be used to display output. One of its most important properties is **Caption**. Using the syntax **label.Caption**, it can display text and numeric data. You can change its caption in the properties window and also at runtime. Please refer to Example 3.1 and Figure 3.1 for the usage of labels.

c) The Command Button

The command button is a very important control as it is used to execute commands. It displays an illusion that the button is pressed when the user clicks on it. The most common event associated with the command button is the Click event, and the syntax for the procedure is:

```
Private Sub Command1_Click ()
Statements
End Sub
```

d) The Picture Box

The Picture Box is one of the controls that is used to handle graphics. You can load a picture during the design phase by clicking on the picture item in the properties window and selecting the picture from the selected folder. You can also load the picture at runtime using the **LoadPicture** method. For example, the following statement will load the picture grape.gif into the picture box.

Picture1.Picture=LoadPicture ("C:\Visual Basic program\Images\grape.gif")

You will learn more about the picture box in future lessons. The image in the picture box is not resizable.

e) The Image Box

The Image Box is another control that handles images and pictures. It functions almost identically to the picture box. However, there is one major difference. The image in an Image Box is stretchable, which means it can be resized. This feature is not available in the Picture Box. Similar to the Picture Box, the LoadPicture method can also be used. For example, this statement loads the picture grape.gif into the image box.

Image1.Picture=LoadPicture ("C:\Visual Basic program\Images\grape.gif")

f) The List Box

The function of the List Box is to present a list of items. The user can click and select items from this list. In order to add items to it, use the **AddItem method**. For example, if you wish to add a number of items to List box 1, you can key in the following statements.

Example 3.2
Private Sub Form_Load ( )
List1.AddItem "Lesson1"
List1.AddItem "Lesson2"
List1.AddItem "Lesson3"
List1.AddItem "Lesson4"
End Sub

The items in the list box can be identified by the **ListIndex** property. The value of the ListIndex for the first item is 0, the second item has a ListIndex 1, and the third item has a ListIndex 2, and so on.

g) The Combo Box

The function of the Combo Box is also to present a list of items. However, the user needs to click on the small arrowhead on the right of the combo box to see the items which are presented in a drop-down list. In order to add items to the list, you can also use the **AddItem method**. For example, if you wish to add a number of items to Combo Box 1, you can key in the following statements

Example 3.3
Private Sub Form_Load ( )
Combo1.AddItem "Item1"
Combo1.AddItem "Item2"
Combo1.AddItem "Item3"
Combo1.AddItem "Item4"
End Sub

h) The Check Box

The Check Box control lets the user select or unselect an option. When the Check Box is checked, its value is set to 1 and when it is unchecked, the value is set to 0. You can include the statements Check1. Value=1 to mark the Check Box and Check1.Value=0 to unmark the Check Box, and use them to initiate certain actions. For example, the program will change the background color of the form to red when the check box is unchecked and it will change to blue when the check box is checked. You will learn about the conditional statement If.... Then....Elseif in later lessons. VbRed and vbBlue are color constants and BackColor is the background color property of the form.

Example 3.4
```
Private Sub Check1_Click ()
If Check1.Value = 0 Then
Form1.BackColor = vbRed
ElseIf Check1.Value = 1 Then
Form1.BackColor = vbBlue
End If
End Sub
```

i) The Option Button

The Option Button also lets the user select one of the choices. However, two or more Option Buttons must work together because if one of the Option Buttons is selected, the other Option Buttons will be unselected. In fact, only one Option Button can be selected at one time. When an option button is selected, its value is set to "True", and when it is unselected, its value is set to "False". In the following example, the shape control is placed in the form together with six Option Buttons. When the user clicks on different option buttons, different shapes will appear. The values of the shape control are 0, 1, 2, 3, 4, and 5 which will make it appear as a rectangle, a square, an oval shape, a rounded rectangle and a rounded square respectively.

Example 3.5
```
Private Sub Option1_Click ()
Shape1.Shape = 0
End Sub
Private Sub Option2_Click()
Shape1.Shape = 1
End Sub
Private Sub Option3_Click()
Shape1.Shape = 2
End Sub
Private Sub Option4_Click()
Shape1.Shape = 3
End Sub
Private Sub Option5_Click()
Shape1.Shape = 4
End Sub
Private Sub Option6_Click()
```

Shape1.Shape = 5
End Sub

j) The Drive List Box

The Drive List Box is used to display a list of drives available in your computer. When you place this control into the form and run the program, you will be able to select different drives from your computer as shown in Figure 3.3:

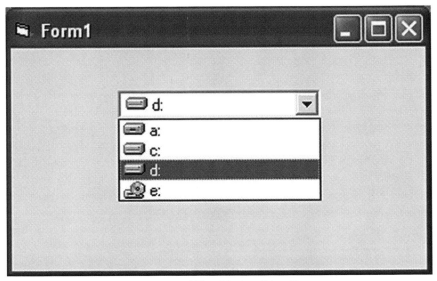

Figure 3.3 The Drive List Box

k) The Directory List Box

The Directory List Box is used to display the list of directories or folders in a selected drive. When you place this control into the form and run the program, you will be able to select different directories from a selected drive in your computer as shown in Figure 3.4:

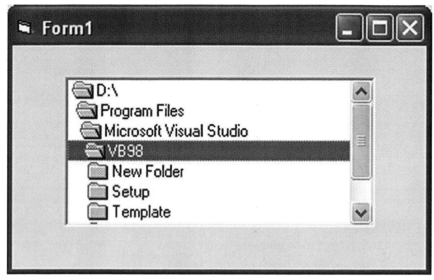

Figure 3.4 The Directory List Box

l) The File List Box

The File List Box is used to display the list of files in a selected directory or folder. When you place this control into the form and run the program, you will be able to see a list of files in a selected directory as shown in Figure 3.5:

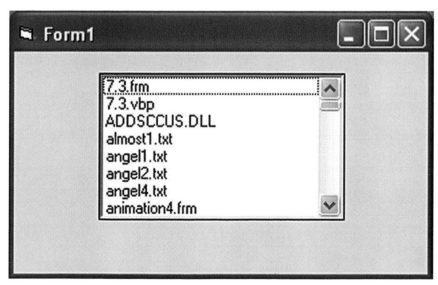

Figure 3.5

*You can coordinate the Drive List Box, the Directory List Box and the File List Box to search for the files you want. This procedure will be discussed in later lessons.

Exercise 3

1. Start a Visual Basic project and set the following properties of the form:
   a. Appearance=Flat
   b. Caption=My First Program
   c. Font=Times New Roman, Font Size=10
   d. Forecolor=White
   e. Backcolor=Blue

2. Insert six shape controls into the form and set their shape properties to rectangle, square, oval, circle, rounded rectangle, and rounded square.

3. Insert two text boxes, one label and one command button, then write the program to compute the product of two numbers that are entered into the text boxes and display the result in the label.

4. Insert a picture control in the form and load a picture from your computer using the LoadPicture Method.

5. Insert a List Box control into the form and add 5 items into the List Box using the AddItem Method.

Lesson 4

Writing the Codes

- Learning about the Visual Basic program structure.
- Setting the properties of the controls at runtime.
- Getting to know some basic syntax.

In lesson 2 and lesson 3, you have learned how to enter program code and run sample Visual Basic programs but without much understanding of the logics of Visual Basic programming. Therefore in this lesson we will tackle a few basic rules about writing Visual Basic program codes.

Each control or object in Visual Basic can usually run many kinds of events or procedures. These events are listed in the dropdown list in the code window which is displayed when you click on the procedures' box after double-clicking on an object (refer to Figure 2.3). Among the events are loading a form, clicking of a command button, pressing a key on the keyboard or dragging an object etc. For each event, you need to write an event procedure so that an action or a series of actions can be performed.

To start writing an event procedure, you need to double-click an object. For example, when you double-click on the command button, the code window will appear showing an event procedure:

Private Sub Command1_Click
(Key in your program code here)
End Sub

You then need to key in the procedure in the space between Private Sub Command1_Click............. End Sub. The program code is made up of a number of statements that set certain properties or trigger some actions. The syntax of Visual Basic's program code is almost like English though not exactly the same, so it is very easy to learn.

The syntax to set the property of an object or to assign certain values to it where **Object** and **Property** are separated by a period is:

Object.Property

For example, the statement **Form1.Show** means to show the form with the name Form1, and **Label1.Visible=true** means Label1 is set to be visible, **Text1.text= "Visual Basic"** is to assign the text Visual Basic to the text box with the name Text1, **Text2.text=100** is to assign a value of 100 to the text box with the name Text2, **Timer1.Enabled=False** is to disable the timer with the name Timer1 and so on. Let's examine a few examples below:

Example 4.1

Private Sub Command1_click
Label1.Visible=False
Label2.Visible=True
Text1.Text="You are correct!"
End sub

Example 4.2

Private Sub Command1_click
Label1.Caption=" Welcome"
Image1.visible=True
End sub

Example 4.3

Private Sub Command1_click
Pictuire1.Show=true
Timer1.Enabled=True
Lable1.Caption="Start Counting"
End sub

In example 4.1, clicking on the command button will make Label1 become invisible and Label2 become visible, and the text "You are correct" will appear in the Text1 textbox. In example 4.2, clicking on the command button will make the caption of Label1 change to "Welcome" and Image1 will become visible. For example 4.3, clicking on the command button will make Picture1 show up, the timer start running and the caption of Label1 change to "Start Counting".

Syntaxes that do not involve the setting of properties are also English-like. Some of the commands are **Print, If...Then....Else.... End If, For...Next, Select Case.....End Select, End** and **Exit Sub.** For example, **Print "Visual Basic"** is to display the text Visual Basic on screen and **End** is to end the program. Other commands will be explained in detail in the coming lessons.

Program codes which involve calculations are very easy to write, as they are similar to mathematics. However, in order to write an event procedure that involves calculations, you need to know the basic arithmetic operators in Visual Basic as they are not exactly the same as the normal operators that we use, except for + and—. For multiplication, we use *****, for division we use /, for raising a number x to the power of n, we use **x ^n** and for square root, we use **Sqr(x).** There are also more advanced mathematical functions such as **Sin, Cos, Tan, Log** etc. Besides that, there are two important functions that are related to arithmetic operations, i.e. the functions **Val** and **Str** where Val is to convert text into a numeric and Str is to convert a numeric into a string. While the function Str is not as vital because Visual Basic can display numeric values as a string implicitly, failure to use Val will result in wrong calculation. Let's examine example 4.4 and example 4.5.

Example 4.4
```
Private Sub Form_Activate()
Text3.text=Text1.text+Text2.text
End Sub
```

Example 4.5
```
Private Sub Form_Activate()
Text3.text=val(Text1.text)+val(Text2.text)
End Sub
```

When you run the program in example 4.4 and enter 12 in the Text1 textbox and 3 in the Text2 textbox, it will give you a result of 123, which is wrong. It is because Visual Basic treats the numbers as strings and so it just joins up the two strings. On the other hand, running example 4.5 will give you the correct result, i.e., 15.

Now we shall write the codes for the cylinder program (the interface is shown in Figure 2.8). First of all, name the text boxes as radius, hght, and volume. To get the values of the various text boxes, use Val(radius.text), Val(hght.Text) and assign them to the variables r and h. In addition, assign the value 22/7 to the variable pi. After that, write the equation v = pi * (r ^ 2) * h to compute the value of the cylinder's volume and then assign it to the variable v. Finally, display the value in the volume textbox using the function Str.

```
Private Sub OK_Click( )
r = Val(radius.Text)
h = Val(hght.Text)
pi = 22 / 7
v = pi * (r ^ 2) * h
volume.Text= Str(v)
End Sub
```

When you run the program, you should be able to see the interface as shown in Figure 2.8. Enter values in the radius box and the height box, and then click OK. The value of the Volume will be displayed in the volume box.

Exercise 4

1. Write a program to compute the area of a triangle.
2. Write a program to calculate the circumference and area of a circle.

Lesson 5

Visual Basic Data

- Getting to know different types of Visual Basic data.
- Rules in naming the Visual Basic variables.
- Declaring variables using the Dim statements.

There are many types of data that we come across in our daily life. For example, we need to handle data such as names, addresses, money, date, stock quotes, statistics etc everyday. Similarly in Visual Basic, we are also going to deal with these kinds of data. However, to be more systematic, Visual Basic divides data into different types.

5.1 Types of Visual Basic Data

a) Numeric Data

Numeric data are data that consist of numbers, which can be computed mathematically with various standard operators such as, add, minus, multiply, divide and so on. In Visual Basic, the numeric data are divided into 7 types, which are summarized in Table 5.1:

Type	Storage	Range of Values
Byte	1 byte	0 to 255
Integer	2 bytes	-32,768 to 32,767
Long	4 bytes	-2,147,483,648 to 2,147,483,648
Single	4 bytes	-3.402823E+38 to to 3.402823E+38
Double	8 bytes	-1.79769313486232E+308 to 1.79769313486232E+308
Currency	8 bytes	-922,337,203,685,477.5808 to 922,337,203,685,477.5807

Table 5.1: Numeric Data Types

b) Non-numeric Data Types

The non-numeric data types are summarized in Table 5.2

Data Type	Storage	Range
String(fixed length)	Length of string	1 to 65,400 characters
String(variable length)	Length + 10 bytes	0 to 2 billion characters
Date	8 bytes	January 1, 100 to December 31, 9999
Boolean	2 bytes	True or False
Object	4 bytes	Any embedded object
Variant(numeric)	16 bytes	Any value as large as Double
Variant(text)	Length+22 bytes	Same as variable-length string

Table 5.2: Nonnumeric Data Types

c) Suffixes for Literals

Literals are values that you assign to data. In some cases, we need to add a suffix behind a literal so that Visual Basic can handle the calculation more accurately. For example, we can use num=1.3089# for a Double data type. Some of the suffixes are displayed in Table 5.3.

Suffix	Data Type
%	Integer
&	Long
!	Single
#	Double
@	Currency

Table 5.3

In addition, we need to enclose string literals within two quotations and date and time literals within two # signs. Strings can contain any type of characters, including numbers. The following are a few examples:

- memberName$="Turban, John."
- TelNumber$="1800-900-888-777"
- LastDay=#31-Dec-00#
- ExpTime=#12:00 am#
- Mark%=90
- profit@=1000.55

It should be noted that in most cases, it is not necessary to use suffixes as long as we declare the variables using the Dim statement.

5.2 Managing Variables

Variables are like mail boxes in the post office. The contents of the variables change every now and then, just like mail boxes. In terms of Visual Basic, variables are areas allocated by the computer memory to hold data. Like the mail boxes, each variable must be given a name. To name a variable in Visual Basic, you have to follow a set of rules.

a) Variable Names

The following are the rules when naming the variables in Visual Basic:

- It must be less than or equal to 255 characters.
- No spacing is allowed.
- It must not begin with a number.
- Periods are not permitted.

Examples of valid and invalid variable names are displayed in Table 5.4:

Valid Name	Invalid Name
My_Car	My.Car
this year	1NewBoy
Long_Name_Can_beUSE	He&HisFather

Table 5.4

b) Declaring Variables

In Visual Basic, one needs to declare the variables before using them by assigning names and data types. You can declare the variables implicitly or explicitly. For example, sum=Text1.text means that the variable sum is declared implicitly and is ready to receive the input in the Text1 textbox. Other examples of implicit declarations are volume=8 and label="Welcome". On the other hand, for explicit declaration, variables are normally declared in the general section of the codes' windows using the Dim statement.

The format is as follows:

Dim variableName as DataType
Example 5.1
Dim password As String
Dim yourName As String
Dim firstnum As Integer
Dim secondnum As Integer
Dim total As Integer
Dim doDate As Date

You may also combine them in one line, separating each variable with a comma, as follows:

Dim password As String, yourName As String, firstnum As Integer.

If the data type is not specified, Visual Basic will automatically declare the variable as a Variant. For string declaration, there are two possible formats, one for the variable-length string and another for the fixed-length string. For the variable-length string, just use the same format as Example 5.1. However, for the fixed-length string, you have to use the format as shown below:

Dim VariableName as String * n,

where n defines the number of characters the string can hold. For example, Dim yourName as String * 10 means yourName can hold no more than 10 Characters.

Exercise 5

1. List out all numeric and non-numeric data types.
2. State the rules in naming the variables.
3. Write five examples of valid variable names.
4. Use the Dim statements to declare three numeric variables and three non-numeric variables.

Lesson 6

Managing Visual Basic Data

- Assigning values to the variables.
- Getting to know various arithmetic operators in Visual Basic.

6.1 Assigning Values to the Variables

After declaring various variables using the Dim statements, we can assign values to those variables. The general format of an assignment is:

Variable=Expression

The variable can be a declared variable or a control property value. The expression could be a mathematical expression, a number, a string, a Boolean value (true or false) etc. The following are some examples:

firstNumber=100
secondNumber=firstNumber-99
userName="John Lyan"
userpass.Text = password
Label1.Visible = True
Command1.Visible = false
Label4.Caption = Text1 textbox.Text
ThirdNumber = Val(usernum1.Text)
total = firstNumber + secondNumber+ThirdNumber

6.2 Arithmetic Operators in Visual Basic

In order to compute input from users and to generate results, we need to use various mathematical operators. In Visual Basic, except for + and -, the symbols for the operators are different from normal mathematical operators, as shown in Table 6.1.

Operator	Mathematical operation	Example
^	Exponential	2^4=16
*	Multiplication	4*3=12
/	Division	12/4=3
Mod	Returns remainder from an integer division	15 Mod 4=3
\	Integer division (discards decimal places)	19\4=4
+ or &	String concatenation	"Out"&"put"="Output"

Table 6.1: Arithmetic Operators

Example 6.1
```
Dim firstName As String
Dim secondName As String
Dim yourName As String

Private Sub Command1_Click()
firstName = Text1.Text
secondName = Text2.Text
yourName = secondName + " " + firstName
Label1.Caption = yourName
End Sub
```

In this example, three variables are declared as string. Variables firstName and secondName will receive their data from the user's input into the Text1 textbox and the Text2 textbox, and the variable yourName will be assigned the data by combining the first two variables. Finally, yourName is displayed on Label1.

Example 6.2
```
Dim number1, number2, number3 as Integer
Dim total, average as variant
Private sub Form_Click
number1=val(Text1.Text)
number2=val(Text2.Text)
number3= val(Text3.Text)
```

```
Total=number1+number2+number3
Average=Total/5
Label1.Caption=Total
Label2.Caption=Average
End Sub
```

In example 6.2, three variables are declared as integers and another two variables are declared as variants. Variant means the variable can hold any numeric data type. The program computes the total and average of the three numbers that are entered into three text boxes.

Example 6.3

```
Dim sellPrice As Currency
Dim costPrice As Currency
Dim profit As Currency

Private Sub Command1_Click ()
sellPrice = Text1.Text
costPrice = Text2.Text
profit = sellPrice—costPrice
Text3.Text = Format (profit, "Currency")
End Sub
```

In example 6.3, three variables namely sellprice, costPrice and Profit are formatted as currency because we are dealing with financial calculations. The output is formatted using the function **Format (profit, "Currency")** which will display Profit in the Text3 textbox in the currency form, i.e. a $ sign and a number with two decimal places as shown in Figure 6.1. We will deal with the function Format again in a later lesson under formatting outputs.

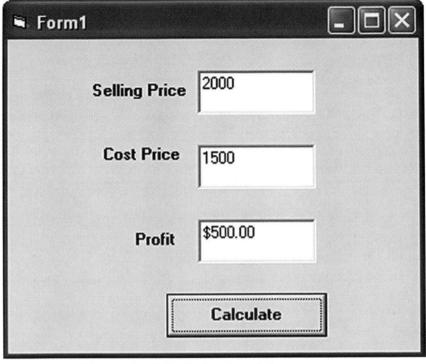

Figure 6.1 Calculation involving currency

In the coming lessons, we will see how to write more complex Visual Basic programs using mathematical operators and equations.

Exercise 6

1. Write down the arithmetic operators in Visual Basic.
2. Write a program to calculate the values of the following arithmetic operations if the users input two numbers M and N into two separate text boxes.
   a) M^N
   b) M/N
   c) M\N
   d) M Mod N

Lesson 7

Controlling Program Flow—Part I

- Getting to know the conditional operators.
- Getting to know the logical operators.
- Using the If.....Then...Else ...Elseif statements.
- Using timers and the Rnd function.

7.1 Conditional Operators

To control the Visual Basic program flow, we can use various conditional operators. Basically, they resemble mathematical operators. Conditional operators are very powerful tools which let the Visual Basic program compare data values and then decide what action to take, whether to execute or terminate the program etc. These operators are shown in Table 7.1.

Operator	Meaning
=	Equal to
>	More than
<	Less than
>=	More than and equal to
<=	Less than and equal to
<>	Not equal to

Table 7.1 Conditional Operators

* You can also compare strings with the above operators. However, there are certain rules to follow:

a. Upper case letters are lesser than lowercase letters

b. "A"< "B"< "C "< "D".......< "Z"

c. Numbers are lesser than letters.

7.2 Logical Operators

In addition to conditional operators, there are a few logical operators that offer added power to the Visual Basic programs. They are shown in Table 7.2:

Operator	Meaning
And	Both sides must be true
Or	One side or other must be true
Xor	One side or other must be true but not both
Not	Negates truth

Table 7.2

7.3 Using If.....Then.....Elseif....Else Statements with Operators

To effectively control the Visual Basic program flow, you can use the If...Then...Else statement together with the conditional operators and logical operators.

The general format for the If...Then...Elseif....Else statement is as follows:

If conditions Then
Visual Basic expressions
Elseif

Visual Basic expressions
Else
Visual Basic expressions
End If

* Any If...Then...Else statements must end with End If. Sometime it is not necessary to use Else.

Example 7.1


```
Private Sub Command1_Click ()
firstnum = Val(Text1.Text)
secondnum = Val(Text2.Text)
total = firstnum + secondnum
If total = Val(Text3.Text) And Val(Text3.Text) <> 0 Then
Label1.Caption="Yes, you are Correct"
Else
Label1.Caption=" Sorry, you're wrong"
End If
End Sub
```


In Example 7.1, the program adds the values entered in the Text1 textbox and the Text2 textbox and compares the answer with the answer entered by the user in the Text3 textbox. If both values are equal, Label1 will display the caption "Yes, you are Correct", otherwise it will show the caption "Sorry, you're wrong".

Example 7.2
```
Dim password As String

Private Sub Command1_Click()
If Text1.Text = password Then
Text1.Visible = False
Label1.Visible = True
Label1.Caption = "Login Successful"
Else
Label1.Visible = True
Label1.Caption = "Login Fail! Please enter your password again"
Text1.Text = ""
```

```
End If
End Sub

Private Sub Form_Load()
password = "1234"
End Sub

Private Sub Text1_Click()
Label1.Visible = False
End Sub
```

In Example 7.2, the program will check whether the password entered by the user matches the password assigned by the Form_Load procedure. If the two passwords match, then the textbox will disappear and the label will display "Login Successful"; otherwise the label will display "Login Fail! Please enter your password again" and the user has to key in the password again. One more thing that you need to do is set the PasswordChar of the Text1 textbox to the character you like (I prefer using * as it is commonly used) in the properties window so that the password entered will be hidden. This program can be used as a login procedure for a database management program as the user needs to enter the password to search for the information stored in a database. The details of how to combine this procedure with the database management program will be discussed later.

Example 7.3

```
'Guess a Number
Dim realNumber As Integer
Dim userNumber As Integer

Private Sub Form_Load()
realNumber = 99
End Sub

Private Sub OK_Click()
userNumber = entry.Text
If userNumber > realNumber Then
hint.Caption = "Your number is too big"
entry.Text = ""
ElseIf userNumber < realNumber Then
hint.Caption = "Your number is too small"
```

```
entry.Text = ""
Else
hint.Caption = "Congratulations, your number is correct"
End If
End Sub
```

Example 7.3 is a 'Guess a Number' program. The user enters a number and the program gives hints whether the number entered is too big or too small. Once the answer is correct, the program will display a congratulatory message. The program uses the If...Then...ElseIf and Else statements together with the conditional operators >, < and = to control the program flow. In this program, the name of the Text1 textbox is renamed as entry and the caption is renamed to display the hint as hint. The statement entry.Text="" is to clear the textbox if the number entered is incorrect so that the user can key in a number again without having to erase the number manually. Notice that the condition userNumber=realNumber is not necessary as the Else statement will handle this condition implicitly.

Example 7.4

This program is a password cracker where it can generate possible passwords and compare each of them with the actual password; and if the generated password is found to be equal to the actual password, login will be successful.

In this program, a timer is inserted into the form and it is used to do the repetitive job of generating the passwords. The password generating procedure is put under the timer1_Timer () event so that the procedure is repeated after every interval. The interval of the timer can be set in its properties window where a value of 1 is 1 millisecond, so a value of 1000 is 1 second which means the smaller the value, the shorter the interval. However, do not set the timer to zero because if you do that, the timer will not start. The Timer1.Enabled property is set to false so that the program will only start generating the passwords after you click on the command button.

Rnd is a Visual Basic function that generates a random number between 0 and 1. Multiplying Rnd by 100 will obtain a number between 0 and 100. Int is a Visual Basic function that returns an integer by ignoring the decimal part of that number. Therefore, Int(Rnd*100) will produce a number between 0 and 99, and the value of Int(Rnd*100)+100 will produce a number between 100 and 199. Randomize timer is an essential statement which ensures that the generated numbers are truly random. Finally, the program uses If...Then...Else to check whether the generated password is equal to the actual password or not; and if they are equal, the password generating process will be terminated by setting the Timer1.Enabled property to false.

The Program

```
Dim password As Integer
Dim crackpass As Integer

Private Sub Command1_Click()
Timer1.Enabled = True
End Sub

Private Sub Form_Load()
password = 123
End Sub

Private Sub Timer1_Timer()
Randomize Timer
crackpass = Int(Rnd * 100) + 100
If crackpass = password Then
Timer1.Enabled = False
Text1.Text = crackpass
Label1.Visible = True
Label1.Caption = "Password Cracked! Login Successful!"

Else
Text1.Text = crackpass
Label1.Visible = True
Label1.Caption = "Please wait..."
End If
End Sub
```

Exercise 7
1.   Write down all the conditional operators.
2.   Write down all the logical operators.

3. Create a simple interactive children word game so that if the answer is correct, the program will display a congratulatory message and when the answer is wrong, the program will ask the child to try again.

4. Write a program to display a person's socio economical status based on his income. For example, if the person's income is less than $1000 per month, his socio economic status may be called poor, if his income is more than $1000 but less than $3000 per month, his socio economic status may be labeled as low income and so on.

Lesson 8

Controlling Program Flow— Part II

- Using the Select Case .... End Select Statement
- Learning more about the usage of the Select Case .... End Select Statement through examples.

8.1 The Select Case .... End Select Statement

In lesson 7, you have learned how to use the conditional statements If.....Then...ElseIf and Else to control the program flow. However, if you have a lot of conditional statements, using If..Then..Else statements could become very messy. For multiple conditional statements, it is always better to use the **Select Case** statement. The structure is shown as follows:

Select Case expression
Case value1
Block of one or more Visual Basic statements
Case value2
Block of one or more Visual Basic Statements
Case value3
Block of one or more Visual Basic statements
Case Else
Block of one or more Visual Basic Statements
End Select

Example 8.1
'To compute examination grades
Dim grade As String
Private Sub txtgrade_Change()
grade = txtgrade.Text

```
Select Case grade
Case "A"
result. Caption = "Distinction"
Case "B"
result.Caption = "Credit"
Case "C"
result.Caption = "Pass"
Case Else
result.Caption = "Fail"
End Select
End Sub
```

In example 8.1, note that the grade is declared as a string, so all the case values such as "A" must be of the String data type. Also note that every select case statement must end with the End Select statement. When the program is run and the user keys in the grade into the text box named as txtgrade, it will look for the case value that matches the input and then display the result on the label named as result. The last statement Case Else means any case other than A, B, C will get the "fail" result.

However, there are a couple of problems in the above program. If the user enters the lower case letters a, b or c and the result will be "fail" because the case values are the uppercase letters A, B, C. In addition, if the user keys in numeric values or other characters other than A, B, C, D, E, F (assuming these are the designated grades), the results will also be "fail".

In order to avoid the above problems, first of all you need to use the function **Ucase** to handle the first problem. The format is **Ucase (txtgrade.Text)**. This will convert the lower case letters to the upper case letters. Secondly, you have to add two additional statements to handle grades D, E, F that are considered as fail and another statement to handle other kinds of inputs that are deemed as invalid data. The statement **Case Is= "D", "E", "F"** will include cases when the grade is D, E or F. The keyword to use here is **Is** and the cases are separated by commas. The last statement which uses the Case Else syntax will deem all other inputs as invalid. It is important for the cases to be exhaustive; i.e. we should take all possible cases into consideration so that no ambiguous results will occur. Example 8.1(b) is the corrected version.

Example 8.2

```
Dim grade As String
Private Sub txtgrade_Change()
grade = UCase(txtgrade.Text)
Select Case grade
Case "A"
result.Caption = "Distinction"
Case "B"
result.Caption = "Credit"
Case "C"
result.Caption = "Pass"
Case Is = "D", "E", "F"
result.Caption = "Fail"
Case Else
result.Caption = "invalid data"
End Select
End Sub
```

Example 8.3

```
Dim mark As Single
Private Sub Compute_Click ()
'Examination Marks
Private Sub mrk_Change()
mark = mrk.Text
Select Case mark
Case 85 To 100
comment.Caption = "Excellent"
Case 70 To 84
comment.Caption = "Good"
Case 60 To 69
comment.Caption = "Above Average"
Case 50 To 59
comment.Caption = "Average"
Case 0 To 49
comment.Caption = "Needs to work harder"
Case Else
comment.Caption = "Values out of range"
End Select
End Sub
```

Example 8.3 is similar to the two preceding examples except that now it handles the numeric data rather than the strings. This program uses the keyword **to** in order to specify the range of values. You can also use Case Is>=n or Case is<n to specify the range of numeric values.

Example 8.4

This example will demonstrate a more complex mathematical application, a simple calculator that can perform four basic arithmetic calculations. In this program, the user just needs to enter two numbers and then select one of the four basic operators from the combo box and obtain the result. The user can perform the four basic calculations at one go for the same pair of numbers just by changing the operators. The program uses two text boxes and a combo box. A combo box is a control that allows the user to select an item from a group of items that are listed in the drop-down list. In order to add a list of items to the combo box, use the following statements and place them under the Private Sub Form_Load procedure:

Combo1.AddItem "+"
Combo1.AddItem "-"
Combo1.AddItem "x"
Combo1.AddItem "÷"

Combo1 is the name of the combo box and AddItem is the method that adds items to the list in the combo box. To identify the items in the list, you can use the ListIndex property of the combo box. The first item will have a ListIndex of 0, the second item will have a ListIndex of 1 and so on. By employing the Select Case.... End Select statements and adding the necessary procedures that perform one of the four basic calculations under each item, the program fulfills its function as a simple calculator.

```
Private Sub Combo1_Click ()
Select Case Combo1.ListIndex
Case 0
Label1 = Val(Text1.Text) + Val (Text2.Text)
Case 1
Label1 = Val(Text1.Text) — Val (Text2.Text)
Case 2
Label1 = Val (Text1.Text) * Val(Text2.Text)
Case 3
Label1 = Val (Text1.Text) / Val (Text2.Text)
End Select
```

End Sub
Private Sub Form_Load ()
Combo1.AddItem "+"
Combo1.AddItem "-"
Combo1.AddItem "x"
Combo1.AddItem "÷"
End Sub

Exercise 8

1. Write a program using the Select Case statement to inform a person about his/her weight status based on the body mass index (BMI) where BMI=body weight in kilograms divided by the square of the height in meters. The weight status is usually shown in the table below

BMI	Weight Status
Below 18.5	Underweight
18.5 – 24.9	Normal
25.0 – 29.9	Overweight
30.0 and Above	Obese

2. Write a program to classify people based on the color they like.

Lesson 9

Looping Part I

- Understanding and using the Do...Loop
- Understanding and using the While...Wend Loop

Very often we need to perform a task repeatedly in order to achieve our objective. This repetitive process is called looping in programming language. Visual Basic allows a procedure to be repeated many times until a condition is met. There are three kinds of loops in Visual Basic, which are **Do.... Loop** , **While... Wend** and **For...Next**.

9.1 Do..... Loop

The structure of a Do Loop command can be written in four different formats as shown below:

a) Do While condition
Block of one or more Visual Basic statements
Loop
b) Do
Block of one or more Visual Basic statements
Loop While condition
c) Do Until condition
Block of one or more Visual Basic statements
Loop
d) Do
Block of one or more Visual Basic statements
Loop Until condition
Example 9.1
Private Sub Form_Activate
Do while counter <10
counter =counter+1

Print Counter
Loop
End Sub

In the above example, the value of the counter will increase by 1 after each loop and it will keep on adding until counter = 10. The values are displayed in Figure 9.1:

Figure 9.1: output of example 9.1

Example 9.2, Example 9.3 and Example 9.4 produce the same result as above.

Example 9.2
Private Sub Form_Activate()
Do
Counter = Counter + 1
Print Counter
Loop Until Counter = 10
End Sub

Example 9.3
Private Sub Form_Activate()
Do Until Counter = 10

```
Counter = Counter + 1
Print Counter
Loop
End Sub
```

Example 9.4
```
Private Sub Form_Activate()
Do
Counter = Counter + 1
Print Counter
Loop While Counter < 10
End Sub
```

Example 9.5
The following example uses the Do...Loop procedure to find the summation of a sequence of numbers, or in mathematical terms, the summation of an arithmetic progression. In this example, we will attempt to find the summation of 1+2+3+4+......+100. In the design stage, you need to insert a list box into the form for displaying the output, named List1. The program uses the AddItem method to populate the list box. The statement List1.AddItem "n" & vbTab & "sum" will display the headings in the list box, where it uses the vbTab function to create a space between the headings n and sum.

Two variables are declared here, where n acts as a counter and sum is the summation of the numbers. The mathematical logic is very simple. Initially, n and sum are set to 0. After the first loop, n=1 and sum=1. After the second loop, n will be equal to 2 (n=1+1) and sum will be equal to 3(sum=1+2); and the next loop will produce the result n=3 and sum=6 (sum=1+2+3). Using Do Until n=100, the program will obtain the summation of 1 to 100. In fact, this program produces the summation at every stage, where the output is displayed in a table form, as shown in Figure 9.2.

```
Dim n, sum As Integer

Private Sub Form_Activate()
List1.AddItem "n" & vbTab & "sum"
Do Until n = 100
n = n + 1
sum = sum + n
List1.AddItem n & vbTab & sum
```

```
Loop
End Sub

Private Sub Form_Load ()
n = 0
sum = 0
End Sub
```

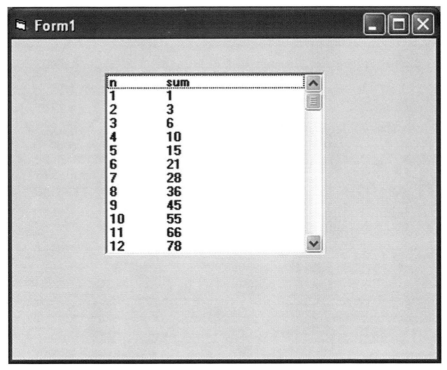

Figure 9.2: The summation of 1 to 100

9.2: Exiting the Do Loop

In section 9.1, we have seen that how a Do loop is terminated when a certain condition is met with one of the four structures i.e. Do Until, Loop Until, Do While and Loop While. Without using the above four controlling statements, the loop will become infinite and it might cause the computer to hang. However, there is yet another way to terminate the loop, that is by using the statements **If....Then** and **Exit Do**. This means that when a condition is met, the program will exit from the loop.

To demonstrate, let's examine example 9.6. You will notice that instead of using the Do Until statement, I have replaced them with the If....Then... and Exit Do statements; and it produces the same result as in example 9.5.

Example 9.6
```
Dim sum, n As Integer

Private Sub Form_Activate()
List1.AddItem "n" & vbTab & "sum"
Do
n = n + 1
Sum = Sum + n
List1.AddItem n & vbTab & Sum
If n = 100 Then
Exit Do
End If
Loop
End Sub

Private Sub Form_Load ()
n = 0
Sum = 0
End Sub
```

9.3 The While....Wend Loop

The structure of a While....Wend Loop is very similar to the Do Loop. It takes the following format:

```
While condition
Statements
Wend
```

The above loop means that while the condition is not met, the loop will go on. The loop will end when the condition is met. Let's examine the program listed in example 9.7 where it produces the same result as Example 9.5 and Example 9.6.

Example 9.7

```
Dim sum, n As Integer
Private Sub Form_Activate ()
List1.AddItem "n" & vbTab & "sum"
While n <> 100
n = n + 1
Sum = Sum + n
List1.AddItem n & vbTab & Sum
Wend
End Sub

Private Sub Form_Load()
n = 0
Sum = 0
End Sub
```

Exercise 9

1. Write a program to add the all the even integers between 101 and 999 using
    a. The Do loop
    b. The While...... Wend Loop
2. Write a program to generate random integers between 1 and 1000 and if the integer 8 appears, the looping will stop and the program will prompt the user to try again.
3. Write a program to print the sentence "I like Visual Basic" twenty times using the While...Wend loop.
4. Write a program to show the geometrical progression in a list box as shown below:

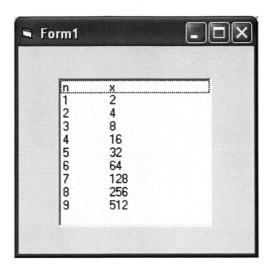

Lesson 10

Looping Part II

- Understanding and using the For...Next Loop
- Understanding the nested Loop

10.1 The For....Next Loop

The For....Next loop is a very useful loop if we intend to have a fixed number of repetitions. It also allows the step increment. If you do not add the step increment, the default increment is 1. The structure of a For....Next loop is:

For counter=startNumber to endNumber (Step increment)
One or more Visual Basic statements
Next counter

* You can actually omit the variable counter and just put in the Next command, but it makes the procedure clearer when you include the variable.

Here are a few examples:

Example 10.1
This program will generate a column of 10 numbers, starting from 1 and ending at 10.
The output is shown in Figure 10.1.

Private Sub Form_Activate()
For counter = 1 To 10
Print Counter

```
Next counter
End Sub
```

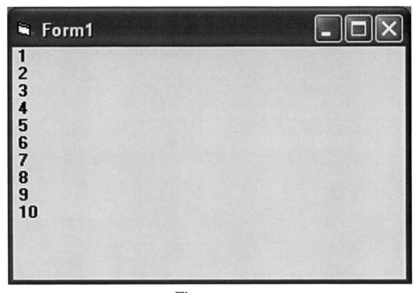

Figure 10.1

Example 10.2
```
Private Sub Form_Activate ()
For counter=0 to 100 step 10
Print counter
Next counter
End Sub
```
This program is similar to the previous example but now the number increases by 10 after every repetition until 100.

Example 10.3
In this example, the number will decrease by 5 after every repetition until it reaches 5.

```
Private Sub Form_Activate
For counter=1000 to 5 step -5
Print counter
Next counter
End Sub
```

Example 10.4

In this example, the program will print the sentence "Hello, Welcome to Visual Basic Tutorial" five times. The output is shown in Figure 10.2

```
Private Sub Form_Activate
For i=1 to 5
print "Hello, Welcome to Visual Basic Tutorial"
next i
End Sub
```

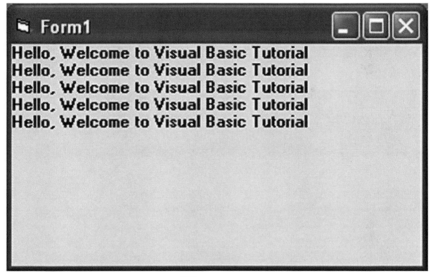

Figure 10.2

10.2 Exiting the For....Next Loop

Sometimes the user might want to get out from the loop before the whole repetitive process is executed. The command to use in this case is **Exit For**. To exit a For....Next Loop, you can place the Exit For statement within the loop. This is normally used together with the If..... Then... statement. Let's examine the following example:

Example 10.5

```
Private Sub Form_Activate ()
```

```
For n = 1 To 10
If n > 6 Then
Exit For
End If
Print n
Next n
End Sub
```

When you run the above program, it will produce the output as shown in Figure 10.3.

The procedure will display the number n until 6. It will not print 7, 8, 9, and 10 because it will exit the loop the moment it reaches 7, as 7 has fulfilled the Exit For condition of n>6. The Exit For command is indeed same as the Exit Do command; they play the same role for exiting a loop.

Figure 10.3: The output of Example 10.5

10.3 The Nested Loop

When you have a loop within a loop, then you have created a nested loop. You can actually have as many loops as you want in a nested loop provided the loops are not the never-ending type. For a nested loop that consists of two loops, the first cycle of the outer loop will be processed first, then it will process the whole repetitive process of the inner loop, then the second cycle of the outer loop will be processed and again the whole repetitive process of the inner loop will be processed. The program will end when the whole cycle of the outer loop is processed.

The Structure of a nested loop is

For counter1=startNumber to endNumber (Step increment)
For counter2=startNumber to endNumber (Step increment)
One or more Visual Basic statements
Next counter2
Next counter1

The outer loop is For....Next counter 1 and the inner loop is For.... Next counter 2, and notice that the inner loop must be enclosed within the outer loop. Let's take a look at example 10.6:

Example 10.6
Private Sub Form_Activate ()
For firstCounter= 1to 5
Print "Hello"
For secondCounter=1 to 4
Print "Welcome to the Visual Basic tutorial"
Next secondCounter
Next firstCounter
Print" Thank you"
End Sub

The output of the above program is shown in Figure 10.6. As the outer loop has five repetitions, it will print the word "Hello" five times. Each time after it prints the word "Hello", it will print four lines of the "Welcome to the Visual Basic tutorial" sentences as the inner loop has four repetitions.

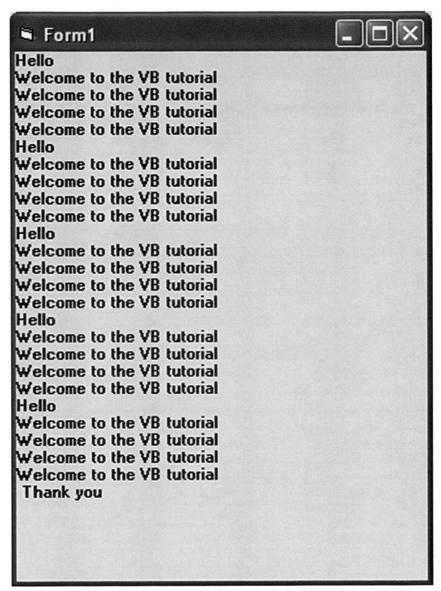

Figure 10.4: The output of Example 10.6

Exercise 10

1. Write a program using the For....Next loop to find the sum of all the numbers from 1 to 100.

2. Write a program using the For....Next loop to find the sum of all the even numbers between 101 and 999.

3. Write a program using the For....Next loop to display the following sequence of numbers 50, 45, 40, 35, 30, 25, 20, 15, 10, 5, 0.

4. Write a program using the For....Next loop to display the following output:

I like
Visual Basic
Visual Basic
Visual Basic
I like
Visual Basic
Visual Basic
Visual Basic

Lesson 11

Visual Basic Functions — Part I

- Understanding the concept of the Visual Basic function
- Learning how to use the MsgBox function
- Learning how to use the InputBox function

11.1 Introduction to Visual Basic Functions

Functions are similar to the normal procedures but the main purpose of the functions is to accept certain input and return a value, which is then passed on to the main program to finish the execution. There are two types of functions, the built-in functions (or internal functions) and the functions created by the programmers.

The general format of a function is:

FunctionName (arguments)

The arguments are values that are passed on to the functions.

In this lesson, we are going to learn two very basic but useful internal functions of Visual Basic, the MsgBox ( ) and the InputBox ( ) functions.

11.2 The MsgBox ( ) Function

The objective of the MsgBox function is to produce a pop-up message box and prompt the user to click on a command button before he /she can continue. This message box format is as follows:

yourMsg=MsgBox (Prompt, Style Value, Title)

The first argument, Prompt, will display the message in the message box. The Style Value determines what type of command button will appear in the message box. Table 11.1 lists the command buttons that can be displayed. The Title argument will display the title of the message board.

Style Value	Named Constant	Button Displayed
0	vbOkOnly	Ok button
1	vbOkCancel	Ok and Cancel buttons
2	vbAbortRetryIgnore	Abort, Retry and Ignore buttons.
3	vbYesNoCancel	Yes, No and Cancel buttons
4	vbYesNo	Yes and No buttons
5	vbRetryCancel	Retry and Cancel buttons

Table 11.1: Style Values and Command Buttons

We can use the named constant in place of an integer for the second argument to make the programs more readable. In fact, Visual Basic6 will automatically show a list of named constants which can be selected. For example, **yourMsg=MsgBox ("Click OK to Proceed", 1, "Startup Menu")** and **yourMsg=Msg ("Click OK to Proceed", vbOkCancel,"Startup Menu")** are the same. YourMsg is a variable that holds values that are returned by the MsgBox ( ) function. The values are determined by the type of buttons being clicked by the users. It has to be declared as Integer data type in the procedure or in the general declaration section. Table 11.2 shows the values, the corresponding named constants and the buttons.

Value	Named Constant	Button Clicked
1	vbOk	Ok button
2	vbCancel	Cancel button
3	vbAbort	Abort button
4	vbRetry	Retry button
5	vbIgnore	Ignore button
6	vbYes	Yes button
7	vbNo	No button

Table 11.2: Return Values and Command Buttons

Example 11.1

In the example, draw three command buttons and a label as shown in Figure 11.1:

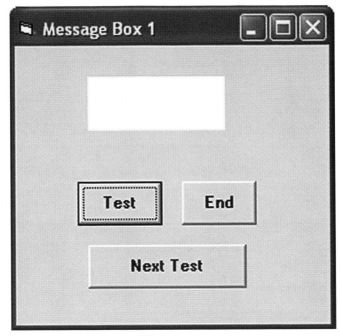

Figure 11.1

The procedure for the test button is shown below:
Private Sub Test_Click ()
Dim testmsg As Integer
testmsg = MsgBox ("Click to test", 1, "Test message")
If testmsg = 1 Then
Display.Caption = "Testing successful"
Else
Display.Caption = "Testing fail"
End If
End Sub

Clicking on the test button will make a message box like the one shown in Figure 11.2 appear. As the user clicks on the OK button, the message "Testing successful" will be displayed and when he/she clicks on the Cancel button, the message "Testing fail" will be displayed.

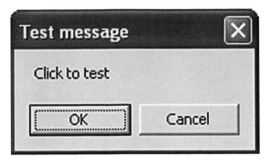

Figure 11.2

To make the message box look more sophisticated, you can add an icon beside the message. There are four types of icons available in Visual Basic as shown in Table 11.3

Value	Named Constant	Icon
16	vbCritical	
32	vbQuestion	
48	vbExclamation	
64	vbInformation	

Table 11.3

Example 11.2
In this example, the following message box will be displayed:

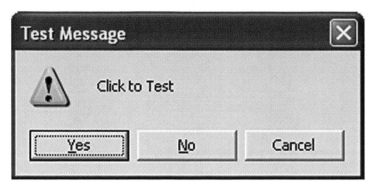

Figure 11.3

You can draw the same interface as in Example 11.1, but modify the codes as follows:

Private Sub test2_Click ()
Dim testMsg2 As Integer
testMsg2 = MsgBox ("Click to Test", vbYesNoCancel + vbExclamation, "Test Message")
If testMsg2 = 6 Then
display2.Caption = "Testing successful"
ElseIf testMsg2 = 7 Then
display2.Caption = "Are you sure?"
Else
display2.Caption = "Testing fail"
End If
End Sub

11.3 The InputBox ( ) Function

An InputBox ( ) function will display a message box where the user can enter a value or a message in the form of text. The format is **myMessage=InputBox (Prompt, Title, default_text, x-position, y-position)**

MyMessage is a variant data type but typically it is declared as a string, which accepts message input by the users. The arguments are explained as follows:

- Prompt—The message displayed in the input box.
- Title—The title of the input box.

- Default-text—The default text that appears in the input field which users can use or change to another message.
- X-position and y-position—the position or the coordinate of the input box.

Example 11.3

The interface of example 11.3 is shown in Figure 11.4:

Figure 11.4

The procedure for the OK button:

Private Sub OK_Click ()

Dim userMsg As String

userMsg = InputBox ("What is your message?", "Message Entry Form", "Enter your message here", 500, 700)

If userMsg <> "" Then

message.Caption = userMsg

Else

message.Caption = "No Message"

End If

End Sub

When the user clicks the OK button, the input box as shown in Figure 11.5 will appear. After the user enters the message and clicks OK, the message will be displayed on the caption, but if he clicks Cancel, "No message" will be displayed.

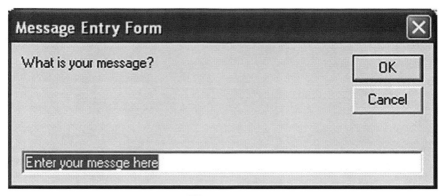

Figure 11.5

Exercise 11

1. Write down the four arguments of the MsgBox function.
2. Write down the six named constants of the MsgBox function.
3. Write down the arguments of the InputBox function.
4. Write a program to verify the password entered into an InputBox by the user.

Lesson12

Visual Basic Functions- Part II

- Getting to know all the mathematical functions in Visual Basic
- Learning how to compute the values of the mathematical functions.

Mathematical functions are very useful and important in programming because very often we need to deal with mathematical concepts in programming such as chance and probability, variables, mathematical logics, calculations, coordinates, time intervals etc. The common mathematical functions in Visual Basic are **Rnd, Sqr, Int, Abs, Exp, Log, Sin, Cos, Tan , Atn, Fix** and **Round.**

12.1 The Rnd Function

Rnd is very useful when we deal with the concept of chance and probability. The Rnd function returns a random value between 0 and 1. In Example 12.1, when you run the program, you will get an output of 10 random numbers between 0 and 1.

Randomize Timer is a vital statement here as it will randomize the process. حيوي

Example 12.1
```
Private Sub Form_Activate
Randomize Timer
For x=1 to 10
Print Rnd
Next x
End Sub
```

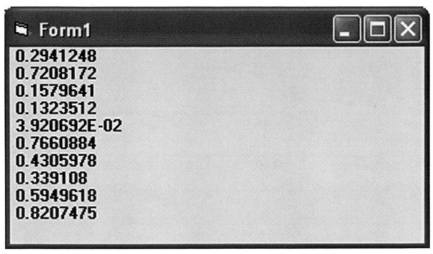

Figure 12.1: The Random Numbers

Random numbers in their original form are not very useful in programming until we convert them to integers. For example, if we need to obtain a random output of 6 integers ranging from 1 to 6, which makes the program behave like a virtual die, we need to convert the random numbers using the format **Int(Rnd*6)+1**. Let's study the following example:

Example 12.2

In this example, Int(Rnd*6) will generate a random integer between 0 and 5 because the function **Int** truncates the decimal part of the random number and returns an integer. After adding 1, you will get a random number between 1 and 6 every time you click the command button. For example, let's say the random number generated is 0.98. Ater multiplying it by 6, it becomes 5.88, the integer function Int(5.88) will convert the number to 5, and after adding 1 you will get 6.

In this example, you place a command button and change its caption to 'roll die'. You also need to insert a label into the form and clear its caption at the designing phase and make its font bigger and bold. Then set the border value to 1 so that it displays a border, and after that set the alignment to center. The statement Label1.Caption=Num means the integer generated will be displayed as the caption of the label. Now, run the program and then click on the roll die button. You will get an output as in Figure 12.2.

```
Dim num as integer
Private Sub Command1_Click ()
Randomize Timer
Num=Int (Rnd*6) +1
Label1.Caption=Num
End Sub
```

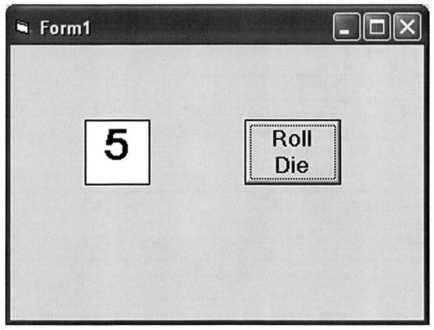

Figure 12.2: A virtual die

Example12.3: A password generator

This is a program that can generate four-digit passwords from 1000 to 9999. The key statement is crackpass = Int (Rnd * 9000) + 1000. For example, when Rnd returns a value of 0, the value of crackpass is 1000; and when Rnd returns 0.9999, the value of Rnd*9000 is 8999.1 and Int (8999.1) will be 8999 and so crackpass will return a value of 9999.

The program is shown below:

'Password Cracker

Dim password As Integer
Dim crackpass As Integer
Dim x As Integer
Private Sub Command1_Click ()
Timer1.Enabled = True
End Sub

Private Sub Form_Load ()
password = 5689
crackpass = 0
End Sub

Private Sub Timer1_Timer()
x = x + 1
If x < 100 Then
Label1.Visible = True
Label1.Caption = "Please wait..."
Randomize Timer
crackpass = Int (Rnd * 9000) + 1000
Text1.Text = crackpass
Else
generate
End If

End Sub

Private Sub generate ()
While crackpass <> password
Randomize Timer
crackpass = Int(Rnd * 9000) + 1000
Text1.Text = crackpass
Wend
Timer1.Enabled = False
Text1.Text = crackpass
Label1.Visible = True
Label1.Caption = "Password Cracked! Login Successful!"
Timer1.Enabled = False

End Sub

12.2 The Numeric Functions

The numeric functions are **Int, Sqr, Abs, Exp, Fix, Round** and **Log.**

a) **Int** is the function that converts a number into an integer by truncating its decimal part and the resulting integer is the largest integer that is smaller than the number. For example, Int(2.4)=2, Int(4.8)=4, Int(-4.6)= -5, Int(0.032)=0 and so on.

b) **Sqr** is the function that computes the square root of a number. For example, Sqr (4)=2, Sqr(9)=3 and etc.

c) **Abs** is the function that returns the absolute value of a number. So Abs (-8) = 8 and Abs (8)= 8.

d) **Exp** of a number x is the value of e^x. For example, Exp (1)=e^1 = 2.7182818284590

e) **Fix** and **Int** are the same if the number is a positive number as both truncate the decimal part of the number and return an integer. However, when the number is negative, it will return the smallest integer that is larger than the number. For example, Fix (-6.34) = -6 while Int (-6.34) = -7.

f) **Round** is the function that rounds up a number to a certain number of decimal places. The Format is Round (n, m) which means to round a number n to m decimal places. For example, Round (7.2567, 2) =7.26

g) **Log** is the function that returns the natural Logarithm of a number. For example,

Log 10= 2.302585.

Example 12.4

This example computes the values of Int(x), Fix(x) and Round(x, n) in a table form. It uses the Do Loop statement and the Rnd function to generate 10 numbers. The statement x = Round (Rnd * 7, 7) rounds a random number between 0 and 7 to 7 decimal places. Using commas in between items will create spaces between them and hence a table of values can be created. The program is shown below and the output is displayed in Figure 12.3.

```
Private Sub Form_Activate ()
n = 1
Print " n", " x", "Int(x)", "Fix(x)", "Round(x, 4)"
Do While n < 11
```

```
Randomize Timer
x = Round (Rnd * 7, 7)
Print n, x, Int(x), Fix(x), Round(x, 4)
n = n + 1
Loop
End Sub
```

n	x	Int(x)	Fix(x)	Round(x, 4)
1	5.35465	5	5	5.3547
2	4.774633	4	4	4.7746
3	3.232793	3	3	3.2328
4	5.999258	5	5	5.9993
5	4.699863	4	4	4.6999
6	3.457101	3	3	3.4571
7	5.326334	5	5	5.3263
8	6.718635	6	6	6.7186
9	4.400786	4	4	4.4008
10	4.354333	4	4	4.3543

Figure 12.3: The output of Example 12.4

الدوال المثلثية

3.3   Trigonometric Functions

3.4

The common trigonometric functions are **Sin, Cos, Tan** and **Atn**.
a)   **Sin** is the function that computes the value of sine of an angle in radian.
b)   **Cos** is the function that computes the value of cosine of an angle in radian.
c)   **Tan** is the function that computes the value of tangent of an angle in radian.
d)   **Atn** is the function that computes the value of arc tangent of an angle in radian.

An angle in degree has to be converted to radian before it can be calculated by the above trigonometric functions. From high school mathematics, we know that π; radian is equivalent to 180°; which means 1 degree is equivalent to π; divided by 180. Therefore, in order

معادل

to convert an angle x from degree to radian, we have to multiply x by $\pi/180$. However, there is a small problem because it is rather difficult to obtain the precise value of π, but fortunately, there is a way to do it in Visual Basic. First of all, we know that an arc tangent of 1 will return the value of 45° which is $\pi/4$ radian. So, to obtain the value of π, just multiply the arc tangent of 1 with 4. Let's examine how all the above calculations can be done in the following examples:

Example 12.5

In this example, the program will display the values of sine, cosine and tangent for various angles in degree between 0° and 360° in a table form. The value of π; is obtained using the equation pi=4*Atn (1). The angle in degree is converted to radian by multiplying the angle by $\pi/180$. Different angles are obtained through the use of For...Next Loop. The program is shown below and the output is shown in Figure 12.4.

```
Private Sub Form_Activate ()
pi = 4 * Atn (1)
Print "angle", "Sin x", "Cos x", "Tan x"
For degree = 0 To 360 Step 30
angle = degree * (pi / 180)
Print degree, Round (Sin (angle), 4), Round (Cos (angle), 4), Round
(Tan (angle), 4)
Next degree
End Sub
```

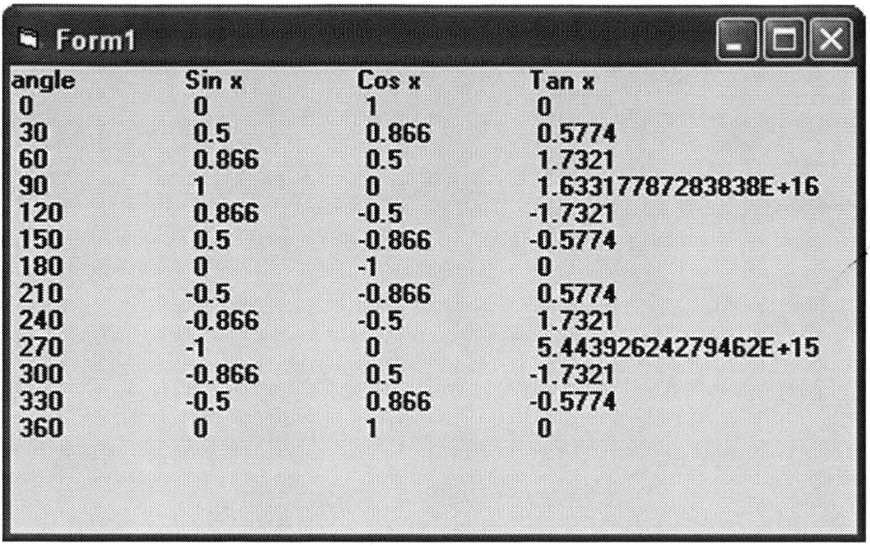

angle	Sin x	Cos x	Tan x
0	0	1	0
30	0.5	0.866	0.5774
60	0.866	0.5	1.7321
90	1	0	1.63317787283838E+16
120	0.866	-0.5	-1.7321
150	0.5	-0.866	-0.5774
180	0	-1	0
210	-0.5	-0.866	0.5774
240	-0.866	-0.5	1.7321
270	-1	0	5.44392624279462E+15
300	-0.866	0.5	-1.7321
330	-0.5	0.866	-0.5774
360	0	1	0

Figure 12.4

Exercise 12

1. Write a program to produce random integers ranging from 20 to 40.

2. Write a program to compute the logarithm of a number and round it up to three decimal places.

3. Write a program to compute the values of sin θ, cos θ and tan θ.

4. Design a simple scientific calculator that can handle various mathematical functions including Log, Abs, Exp, sine, cosine, tangent, Arc tangent, square root and etc.

Lesson13

Visual Basic Functions Part III
Formatting Output

- Understanding the usage of the Tab function.
- Understanding the usage of the Space function.
- Understanding the usage of the Format function.

Formatting output is a very important part of programming so that the data can be presented systematically and clearly to the users. Data in Figure 12.3 and Figure 12.4 were presented fairly systematically through the use of commas and some of the functions like Int, Fix and Round. However, to have better control of the output format, we can use a number of formatting functions in Visual Basic.

The four important formatting functions in Visual Basic are **Tab, Space**, and **Format**.

13.1 The Tab function

The format of the Tab function is

Tab (n); x

The item x will be displayed at a position that is n spaces from the left border of the output form. There must be a semicolon in between Tab and the items you intend to display (Visual Basic will actually do it for you automatically).

Example 13.1

Private Sub Form_Activate()

Print "I"; Tab(5); "like"; Tab(10); "to"; Tab(15); "learn"; Tab(25); "Visual Basic"

Print

Print Tab(10); "I"; Tab(15); "like"; Tab(20); "to"; Tab(25); "learn"; Tab(35);

```
"Visual Basic"
Print
Print Tab(15); "I"; Tab(20); "like"; Tab(25); "to"; Tab(30); "learn";
Tab(40);
"Visual Basic"
End Sub
```

The output of the above example is shown in Figure 13.1. The extra Print statements that do not seem to print anything actually create a space between two lines.

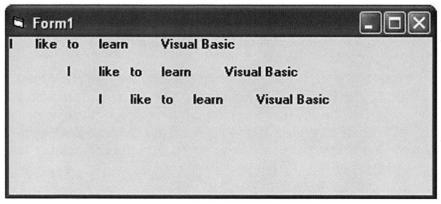

Figure 13.1: The output using the Tab function

Example 13.2:
This example will generate a multiplication table.

```
Private Sub Form_Activate ()
For x = 1 To 10
Print Tab (2); "2" & "x" & Str(x) & "=" & Str (2 * x) _
; Tab (14); "3" & "x" & Str(x) & "=" & Str (3 * x) _
; Tab (26); "4" & "x" & Str(x) & "=" & Str (4 * x) _
; Tab (38); "5" & "x" & Str(x) & "=" & Str (5 * x) _
; Tab (50); "6" & "x" & Str(x) & "=" & Str (6 * x) _
; Tab (62); "7" & "x" & Str (x) & "=" & Str (7 * x) _
; Tab (74); "8" & "x" & Str (x) & "=" & Str (8 * x) _
; Tab (86); "9" & "x" & Str (x) & "=" & Str (9 * x) _
; Tab (98); "10" & "x" & Str (x) & "=" & Str (10 * x) _
Next x
End Sub
```

In this program, each column in the output form is separated by 12 spaces. Str (n) is a function that will convert a number to a string (or text), and the sign "&" is used to join two strings. Str needs to be used here because all the items are taken to be strings.

Notice that "x" and Str(x) are different as "x" will display the letter x while Str(x) is considered as a string and displays the number x. The output is shown in Figure 13.2:

Form1									
2x 1= 2	3x 1= 3	4x 1= 4	5x 1= 5	6x 1= 6	7x 1= 7	8x 1= 8	9x 1= 9	10x 1= 10	
2x 2= 4	3x 2= 6	4x 2= 8	5x 2= 10	6x 2= 12	7x 2= 14	8x 2= 16	9x 2= 18	10x 2= 20	
2x 3= 6	3x 3= 9	4x 3= 12	5x 3= 15	6x 3= 18	7x 3= 21	8x 3= 24	9x 3= 27	10x 3= 30	
2x 4= 8	3x 4= 12	4x 4= 16	5x 4= 20	6x 4= 24	7x 4= 28	8x 4= 32	9x 4= 36	10x 4= 40	
2x 5= 10	3x 5= 15	4x 5= 20	5x 5= 25	6x 5= 30	7x 5= 35	8x 5= 40	9x 5= 45	10x 5= 50	
2x 6= 12	3x 6= 18	4x 6= 24	5x 6= 30	6x 6= 36	7x 6= 42	8x 6= 48	9x 6= 54	10x 6= 60	
2x 7= 14	3x 7= 21	4x 7= 28	5x 7= 35	6x 7= 42	7x 7= 49	8x 7= 56	9x 7= 63	10x 7= 70	
2x 8= 16	3x 8= 24	4x 8= 32	5x 8= 40	6x 8= 48	7x 8= 56	8x 8= 64	9x 8= 72	10x 8= 80	
2x 9= 18	3x 9= 27	4x 9= 36	5x 9= 45	6x 9= 54	7x 9= 63	8x 9= 72	9x 9= 81	10x 9= 90	
2x 10= 20	3x 10= 30	4x 10= 40	5x 10= 50	6x 10= 60	7x 10= 70	8x 10= 80	9x 10= 90	10x 10= 100	

Figure 13.2 The multiplication table

13.2 The Space function

The **Space** function is very closely linked to the Tab function. However, there is a minor difference. While Tab (n) means the item is placed n spaces from the left border of the screen, the Space function specifies the number of spaces between two consecutive items. For example, the procedure will display the words Visual and Basic separated by 10 spaces.

```
Private Sub Form_Activate ()
Print "Visual"; Space (10); "Basic"
End Sub
```

Example 13.3

Example 13.3 is a program that produces the same multiplication table as the previous example but the Tab function is replaced by the Space function. The output is shown in Figure 13.3. Notice that the alignments of the columns are totally off. Therefore, it is normally better to use the Tab function rather than the Spaces function if we want a uniform display of the items in a table.

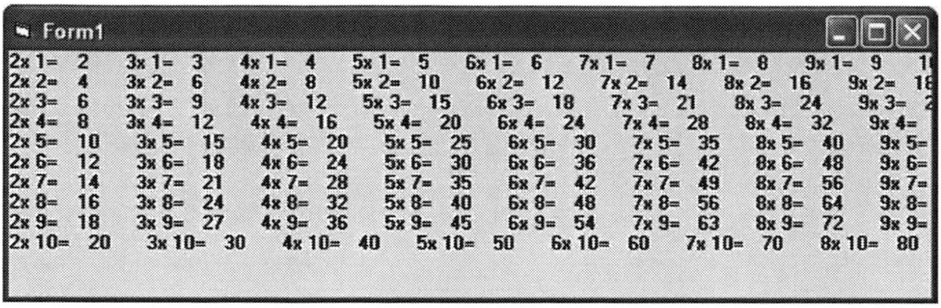

Figure 13.3

Private Sub Form_Activate ()
For x = 1 To 10
Print "2" & "x" & Str(x) & "=" & Space (2); Str(2 * x) _
; Space (6); "3" & "x" & Str(x) & "=" & Space (2); Str (3 * x) _
; Space (6); "4" & "x" & Str(x) & "=" & Space (2); Str (4 * x) _
; Space (6); "5" & "x" & Str(x) & "=" & Space (2); Str(5 * x) _
; Space (6); "6" & "x" & Str(x) & "=" & Space (2); Str(6 * x) _
; Space (6); "7" & "x" & Str(x) & "=" & Space (2); Str(7 * x) _
; Space (6); "8" & "x" & Str(x) & "=" & Space (2); Str(8 * x) _
; Space (6); "9" & "x" & Str(x) & "=" & Space (2); Str(9 * x) _
; Space (6); "10" & "x" & Str(x) & "=" & Space (2); Str(10 * x) _
Next x
End Sub

13.3 The Format function

The **Format** function is a very powerful formatting function which can display the numeric values in various forms. There are two types of Format functions. One of them is the built-in or predefined format while another one can be defined by the users.

(i) The format of the predefined Format function is

Format (n, "style argument")

where n is a number and the list of style arguments is given in Table 13.1.

Style argument	Explanation	Example
General Number	Displays the number without having separators between thousands.	Format(8972.234, "General Number")=8972.234
Fixed	Displays the number without having separators between thousands and rounds it up to two decimal places.	Format(8972.2, "Fixed")=8972.23
Standard	Displays the number with separators between thousands and rounds it up to two decimal places.	Format(6648972.265, "Standard")= 6,648,972.27
Currency	Displays the number with the dollar sign in front, has separators between thousands, and rounds it up to two decimal places.	Format(6648972.265, "Currency")= $6,648,972.27
Percent	Converts the number to percentage form, displays a % sign and rounds it up to two decimal places.	Format(0.56324, "Percent")=56.32 %

Table 13.1 List of style arguments

Example 13.4
Private Sub Form_Activate ()
Print Format (8972.234, "General Number")
Print Format (8972.2, "Fixed")
Print Format (6648972.265, "Standard")
Print Format (6648972.265, "Currency")
Print Format (0.56324, "Percent")
End Sub

Figure 13.4 The output of Example 13.4

(ii) The format of the user-defined Format function is:
Format (n, "user's format")
Although it is known as user-defined format, we still need to follow certain formatting styles. Examples of user-defined formatting style are listed in Table 13.2:

Example	Explanation	Output
Format(781234.57,"0")	Rounds to a whole number without separators between thousands.	781235
Format(781234.57,"0.0")	Rounds to 1 decimal place without separators between thousands.	781234.6
Format(781234.576,"0.00")	Rounds to 2 decimal places without separators between thousands.	781234.58
Format(781234.576,"#,##0.00")	Rounds to 2 decimal places with separators between thousands.	781,234.58
Format(781234.576,"$#,##0.00")	Shows dollar sign and rounds to 2 decimal places with separators between thousands.	$781,234.58
Format(0.576,"0%")	Converts to percentage form without decimal places.	58%
Format(0.5768,"0.00%")	Converts to percentage form with 2 decimal places.	57.68%

Table13.2: User-Defined format

Example 13.5
Private Sub Form_Activate ()
Print Format (781234.57, "0")
Print Format (781234.57, "0.0")
Print Format (781234.576, "0.00")
Print Format (781234.576, "#,##0.00")
Print Format (781234.576, "$#,##0.00")
Print Format (0.576, "0 %")
Print Format (0.5768, "0.00 %")
End Sub

Example 13.5 demonstrates some of the user-defined formatting. The output is shown in Figure 13.5:

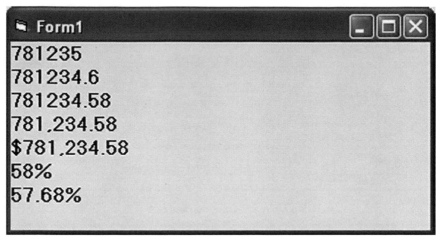

Figure 13.5: The output of user-defined formatting

13.4 Formatting date and time

Date and time can be formatted using predefined formats and also user-defined formats. The predefined formats of date and time are shown in Table 13.3:

Format	Explanation
Format (Now, "General date")	Formats the current date and time.
Format (Now, "Long Date")	Displays the current date in long format.
Format (Now, "Medium Date")	Displays the current date in medium format
Format (Now, "Short date")	Displays the current date in short format
Format (Now, "Long Time")	Display the current time in long format.
Format (Now, "Medium Time")	Display the current time in medium format.
Format (Now, "Short Time")	Display the current time in short format.

Table 13.3 Predefined formats of date and time

Example 13.6

This program will create a clock that can display the date and time in different formats. In order to make the clock actually work according to real time, you need to insert the timer control into the form and enter the formatting procedure in the timer subprogram. In addition, you must set the time interval in the timer's properties window to 1000 so that it is equal to 1 second. You will also need to insert a few labels to display the date and time in different formats. The general method to display data or time on a label is Label1.Caption=date and Label1. Caption=Time. However, in order to format the output, you need to use the formats shown in this example.

```
Private Sub Timer1_Timer()
Label3.Caption = Format (Now, "General Date")
Label5.Caption = Format (Now, "Long Date")
Label8.Caption = Format (Now, "Medium Date")
Label1.Caption = Format (Now, "Long Time")
Label9.Caption = Format (Now, "Short Time")
Label12.Caption = Format (Now, "Medium Time")
End Sub
```

The output is displayed in Figure 13.6:

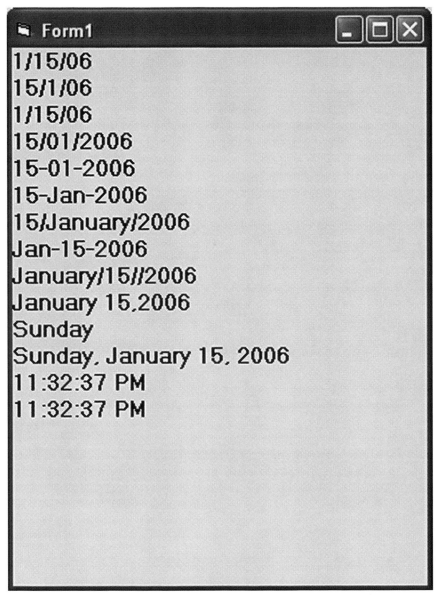

Figure 13.6: Date and Time in different formats

You can also format date and time according to user-defined formats. The user-defined formats for the date involve the use of the d, m and y letters while time format use Hh: Nn: Ss AM/PM and "ttttt". Some of the formats are shown in Table 13.4:

Format	Explanation
Format (Now, "m/d/yy")	Displays a single digit month followed by a single digit day and two-digit year separated by slashes.
Format(Now, "dd/mm/yyyy")	Displays a two-digit day followed by a two-digit month and four-digit year separated by slashes.
Format(Now, "dd-mmm-yyyy")	Displays a two-digit day followed by an abbreviated month name and a four-digit year separated by dashes.
Format(Now, "dd-mmmm-yyyy")	Displays a two-digit day followed by the month name and a four-digit year separated by dashes.
Format(Now, "Hh:Nn:Ss AM/PM")	Displays the current time in a two-digit hour, two-digit minute and two-digit second. It also includes the AM/PM indicator.
Format(Now, "ttttt")	Displays the current time in a two-digit hour, two-digit minute and two-digit second. It also includes the AM/PM indicator.
Format(Now, "dddd")	Displays the current day name.
Format(Now, "dddddd")	Displays the current day name and date.

Table 13.4 Date and Time Formats

Example 13.7
This example displays various formats of Date and Time. The output is shown in Figure 13.7.

```
Private Sub Form_Activate ()
Print Format (Now, "m/d/yy")
Print Format (Now, "d/m/yy")
Print Format (Now, "dd-mm-yyyy")
```

```
Print Format (Now, "dd-mmm-yyyy")
Print Format (Now, "dd/mmmm/yyyy")
Print Format (Now, "mmm-dd-yyyy")
Print Format (Now, "mmmm/dd//yyyy")
Print Format (Now, "mmmm dd, yyyy")
Print Format (Now, "dddd")
Print Format (Now, "dddddd")
Print Format (Now, "Hh: Nn: Ss AM/PM")
Print Format (Now, "ttttt")
End Sub
```

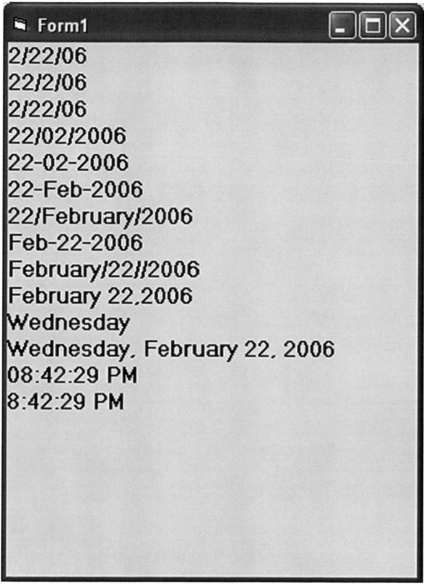

Figure 13.7 Date and Time in different formats

Exercise 13

1. Explain the difference between the Tab and the Space functions and write a program to support your explanation.
2. Write down five style arguments of the Format function and write a program to illustrate these styles.

3. Create a digital clock in Visual Basic that uses three different time formats.

4. Write a program to compute the percentage of price increment of a certain goods based on the new price and the old price. Display the answer in percentage form using the Format function.

Lesson 14

Visual Basic Functions Part IV
Manipulating Strings

- Learning the usage of various strings manipulating functions such as Len, Right, Left, Mid, Trim, Ltrim, Rtrim, Ucase, Lcase, Instr, Val, Str etc, Chr and Asc.

14.1 The Len Function

The Len function returns an integer value which is the length of a phrase or a sentence, including the empty spaces. The format is:
Len ("Phrase")
For example:
Len (VisualBasic) = 11 and Len (welcome to Visual Basic tutorial) = 22

The Len function can also return the number of digits or memory locations of a number that is stored in the computer. For example,
Private sub Form_Activate ( )
X=sqr (16)
Y=1234
Z#=10#
Print Len(x), Len(y), and Len (z)
End Sub
will produce the output 1, 4, 8. The reason why the last value is 8 is because z# is a double precision number and so it is allocated more memory spaces.

14.2 The Right Function
The Right function extracts the right portion of a phrase. The format is

Right ("Phrase", n)
where n is the starting position from the right of the phase where the portion of the phrase is going to be extracted. For example:
Right ("Visual Basic", 4) = asic

14.3 The Left Function

The Left function extracts the left portion of a phrase. The format is

Left ("Phrase", n)
where n is the starting position from the left of the phase where the portion of the phrase is going to be extracted. For example:
Left ("Visual Basic", 4) = Visu

14.4 The Ltrim Function

The Ltrim function trims the empty spaces of the left portion of the phrase. The format is

Ltrim("Phrase")
.For example:
Ltrim (" Visual Basic", 4) = Visual Basic

14.5 The Rtrim Function

The Rtrim function trims the empty spaces of the right portion of the phrase. The format is

Rtrim("Phrase")
.For example:
Rtrim ("Visual Basic ", 4) = Visual Basic

6.6   The Trim function

6.7

The Ttrim function trims the empty spaces on both sides of the phrase. The format is

Trim ("Phrase")
.For example:
Trim (" Visual Basic ") = Visual Basic

14.7 The Mid Function

The **Mid** function extracts a substring from the original phrase or string. The format is

Mid (phrase, position, n)

where position is the starting position of the phrase from which the extraction process will start and n is the number of characters to be extracted. For example:

Mid ("Visual Basic", 3, 6) = ual Bas

14.8 The InStr function

The **InStr** function looks for a phrase that is embedded within the original phrase and returns the starting position of the embedded phrase. The format is

Instr (n, original phase, embedded phrase)

where n is the position where the Instr function will begin to look for the embedded phrase. For example

Instr (1, "Visual Basic"," Basic") =8

14.9 The Ucase and the Lcase functions

The **Ucase** function converts all the characters of a string to capital letters. On the other hand, the **Lcase** function converts all the characters of a string to small letters. For example,

Ucase ("Visual Basic") =Visual Basic

Lcase ("Visual Basic") =Visual Basic

14.10 The Str and Val functions

The **Str** is the function that converts a number to a string while the **Val** function converts a string to a number. These two functions are important when we need to perform mathematical operations.

14.11 The Chr and the Asc functions

The **Chr** function returns the string that corresponds to an ASCII code while the **Asc** function converts an ASCII character or symbol to the corresponding ASCII code. ASCII stands for "American Standard Code for Information Interchange". Altogether there are 255 ASCII codes and as many ASCII characters. Some of the characters may not be displayed as they may represent some actions such as the pressing of a key or beeping. The format of the Chr function is

Chr(charcode)

and the format of the Asc function is

Asc (Character)

The following are some examples:

Chr(65)=A, Chr(122)=z, Chr(37)=% , Asc("B")=66, Asc("&")=38

Example 14.1

This is a program that utilizes some of the functions mentioned in this lesson.

The output is shown in Figure 14.1.

```
Private Sub Form_Activate ()
Print Len ("Visual Basic")
Print Right ("Visual Basic", 4)
Print Left ("Visual Basic", 4)
Print LTrim(" Visual Basic")
Print LTrim("Visual Basic ")
Print Trim(" Visual Basic ")
Print InStr (5, " Visual ", " ")
Print InStr (6, Trim$(" Visual Basic "), " ")
Print Mid ("Visual Basic", 3, 6)
Print InStr (1, "Visual Basic", "Basic")
End Sub
```

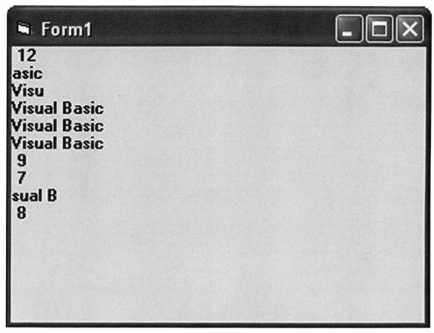

Figure 14.1

Exercise 14

1. List the functions which can be used to manipulate strings and write a program to illustrate these functions.

2. Write a program to compute the ASCII codes that correspond to the characters a—z and A—Z using the Chr function.

Lesson15

Visual Basic Functions Part V- Creating Your Own Functions

• Learning how to create your own functions.

The general format of a function is as follows:

Function functionName (Arg As dataType,..........) As dataType
    Statements
End Function

You can place the word Public or Private in front of Function. Public indicates that the function is applicable to the whole program while Private indicates that the function is only applicable to a certain module or procedure.

Example 15.1
The example shows a function that can be used to calculate the area of a triangle based on the length of its base and its height. The function is:

Private Function area (base As Variant, height As Variant) As Variant
    area = (base * height) / 2
End Function

After you have created the function, you can call it under a procedure such as

Private Sub Command1_Click ()
Label4.Caption = area (Text1.Text, Text2.Text)
End Sub
When the user enters the values into the text boxes and clicks the

command button, the area of the triangle will be displayed in Label4. The output is shown in Figure 15.1:

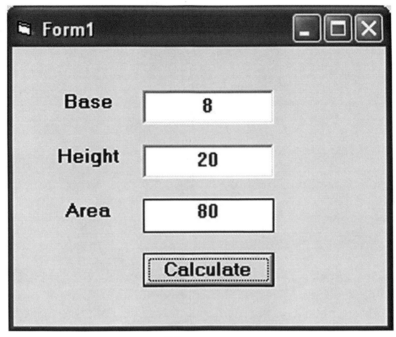

Figure 15.1

Example 15.2
This example illustrates a function that can be used to calculate the profit margin based on the formula

$$\text{Profit Margin} = \frac{\text{Selling Price - Cost Price}}{\text{Selling Price}}$$

The function to compute the profit margin and present it in the percentage form is

```
Private Function PM (SP As Variant, CP As Variant)
PM = Format ((SP—CP) / SP, "Percent")
End Function
```

and the procedure to call the function is

```
Private Sub Command1_Click ()
SP = SPTxt
CP = CPTxt
PMLbl = PM (SP, CP)
End Sub
```

The program will read the values from text boxes and display the result on the label with the name PMLbl. The output is shown in Figure 15.2:

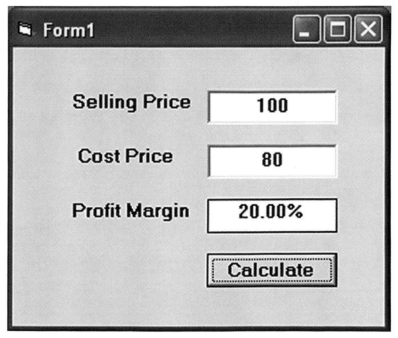

Figure 15.2 The Profit Margin Calculator

Example 15.3

In this example, a user can calculate the future value of a certain amount of money he has today based on the interest rate and the number of years from now (supposing he will invest this amount of money in a bank). The calculation is based on the compound interest rate.

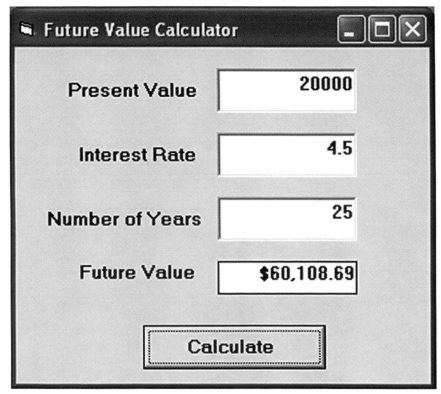

Figure 15.3 The Future Value Calculator

Public Function FV (PV As Variant, i As Variant, n As Variant) As Variant
'Formula to calculate Future Value (FV)
'PV denotes Present Value
FV = PV * (1 + i / 100) ^ n
End Function

Private Sub compute_Click ()
'This procedure will calculate Future Value
Dim FutureVal As Currency
Dim PresentVal As Currency
Dim interest As Variant
Dim period As Variant
PresentVal = PV.Text
interest = rate.Text
period = years.Text

```
FutureVal = FV (PresentVal, interest, period)
Label5.Caption = Format (FutureVal, "currency")
End Sub
```

Example 15.4

The following program will automatically compute examination grades based on the marks that a student obtained.

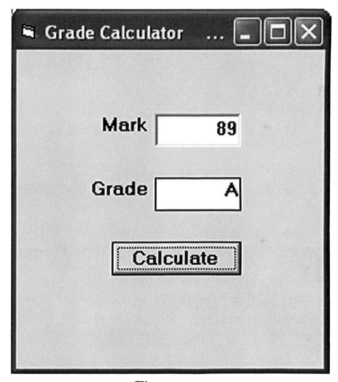

Figure 15.4

```
Private Sub Command1_Click ()
mark = Text1.Text
Label3.Caption = grade (mark)
End Sub
```

```
Private Function grade(mark As Variant) As String
Select Case mark
Case Is >= 80
grade = "A"
```

```
Case Is >= 70
grade = "B"
Case Is >= 60
grade = "C"
Case Is >= 50
grade = "D"
Case Is >= 40
grade = "E"
Case Else
grade = "F"
End Select
End Function
```

Example 15.5

This is a program that can calculate the body mass index, or BMI of a person based on the body weight in kilograms and the body height in meters. BMI can be calculated using the formula

$$\frac{\text{weight}}{\text{height}^2}$$

The program is illustrated below and the output is shown in Figure 15.5:

```
Private Sub Command1_Click ()
Label4.Caption = BMI (Text1.Text, Text2.Text)
End Sub

Private Function BMI (height, weight)
BMIValue = (weight) / (height ^ 2)
BMI = Format (BMIValue, "0.00")
End Function
```

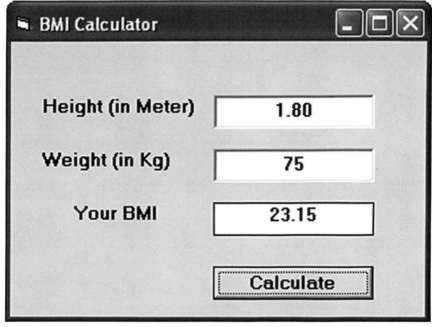

Figure 15.5 BMI calculator

Exercise 15

1. Write a program to compute the area of a rectangle using a user-defined function.
2. Write a program to compute the volume of a cylinder using a user-defined function.
3. Create a user-defined function to calculate the average speed of a car using the formula

$$\text{Average Speed} = \frac{\text{Total Distance Travelled}}{\text{Total Time Taken}}$$

4. Create a user-defined function to calculate the present value that needs to be invested in order to obtain a certain sum of money after a certain number of years based on a certain interest rate per annum.

Lesson 16

Creating Visual Basic Functions for MS Excel

- Learning how to create user-defined functions in MS-Excel using Microsoft Excel Visual Basic Editor.

16.1 The Need to Create User-Defined Functions in MS-Excel

You can create your own functions to supplement the built-in functions in Microsoft Excel spreadsheet which are quite limited. These functions could be very useful and powerful if you know how to program them properly. One of the main reasons we need to create user-defined functions is to customize the spreadsheet environment for individual needs. For example, the user might need a function that could calculate commissions based on the sales volume, which is quite difficult if not impossible by using the built-in functions alone. Let's look at the table below:

Sales Volume($)	Commissions
<500	3%
<1000	6%
<2000	9%
<5000	12%
>5000	15%

Table 16.1: Commissions Payment Table

In the above table, if a salesman attains a sale volume of $6000, he will be paid $6000x12%=$720.00. A Visual Basic function to calculate the commissions can be written as follows:

```
Function Comm (Sales_V As Variant) as Variant
If Sales_V <500 Then
Comm=Sales_V*0.03
Elseif Sales_V>=500 and Sales_V<1000 Then
Comm=Sales_V*0.06
Elseif Sales_V>=1000 and Sales_V<2000 Then
Comm=Sales_V*0.09
Elseif Sales_V>=200 and Sales_V<5000 Then
Comm=Sales_V*0.12
Elseif Sales_V>=5000 Then
Comm=Sales_V*0.15
End If
End Function
```

16.2 Using Microsoft Excel Visual Basic Editor

To create User Defined functions in MS Excel, click on tools, select macro and then click on Visual Basic Editor as shown in Figure 16.1:

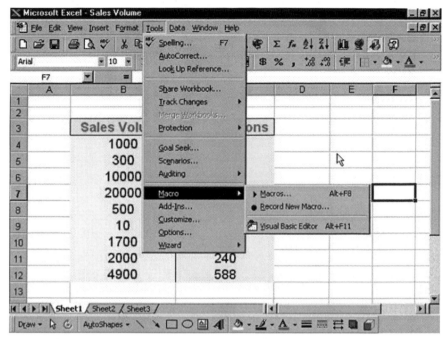

Figure 16.1: Inserting MS_Excel Visual Basic Editor

Upon clicking the Visual Basic Editor, the Visual Basic Editor windows will appear as shown in Figure 16.2. To create a function, type in the function as illustrated in section 16.1 above, save the file and then return to the Excel windows.

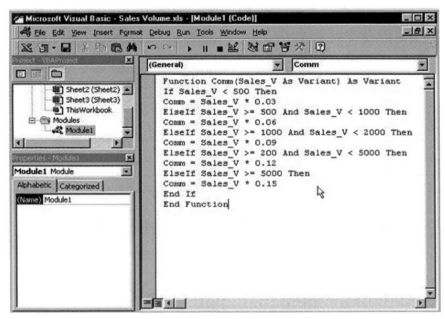

Figure 16.2: The Visual Basic Editor

In the Excel windows, type in the titles Sales Volume and Commissions in any two cells. By referring to Figure 16.3, key in the Comm function at cell C4 and by referencing the value in cell B4, using the format Comm (B4). Any value which appears in cell B4 will pass the value to the Comm function in cell C4. For the rest of the rows, just copy the formula by dragging the bottom-right corner of cell C4 to the required cells and a nice and neat table that shows the commissions will automatically appear. It can also be updated at any time.

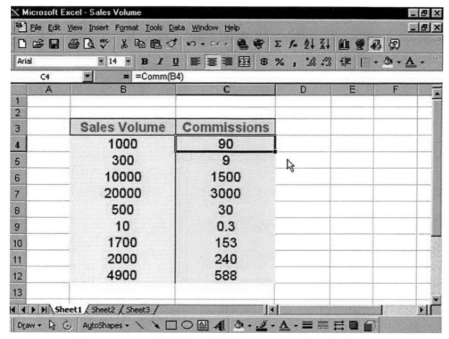

Figure 16.3: MS Excel Windows- Sales Volume

Exercise 16

1. Write a function in MS Excel that computes the grades of the examination scores.
2. Write a function in MS Excel to compute the health status of the patients based on their blood pressures.
3. Write a function in MS Excel to compute the performance of the staff based on the monthly sales quotas achieved.

Lesson 17

Arrays Part I

- Understanding the concept of an array.
- Learning how to declare an array.
- Learning how to create a control array.

17.1 Introduction to Array

When we work with a single item, we only need to use one variable. However, if we have to deal with a list of items which are of similar type, we need to declare an array of variables instead of using a variable for each item. For example, if we need to enter one hundred names, instead of declaring one hundred different variables, we need to declare only one array. By definition, an array is a group of variables with the same data type and name. We differentiate each item in the array by using subscript, the index value of each item, for example name (1), name (2), name (3) ....etc.

17.2 Declaring Arrays

We can use Public or Dim statements to declare an array like the way we declare a single variable. The Public statement declares an array that can be used throughout an application while the Dim statement declares an array that can be used only in a local procedure.

The general format to declare an array is as follows:
i) **Dim arrayName(subs) as dataType**
ii) **Public arrayName(subs) as dataType**

'Subs' indicates the subscript of the last element in the array, instead of the number of elements in the array. This is because Visual Basic assigns a subscript of 0 to the first element rather than 1. For example, Dim book (9) will declare an array which consists of 10 elements, i.e. book(0), book(1), book(2), book(3), book(4), book(5), book(6), book(7), book(8) and book(9).

In order to assign 1 to the subscript of the first element in an array, you need to include the statement **Option Base 1** in the declaration area. With Option Base 1, Dim CusName (10) as String will declare an array that consists of 10 elements, starting from CusName (1) to CusName (10). Otherwise, there will be 11 elements in the array starting from CusName (0) through to CusName (10). In addition, using Dim Count (100 to 500) as Integer will declare an array that consists of elements starting from Count (100) and ending at Count (500).

Example 17.1

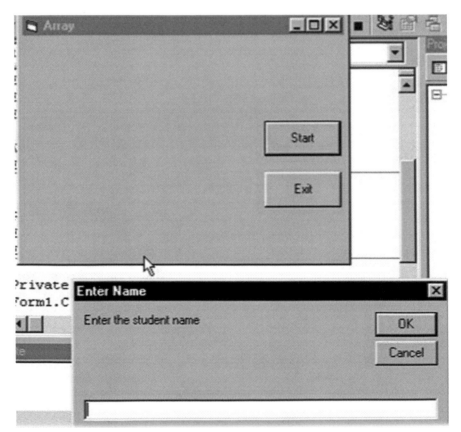

Figure 17.1

Dim studentName(10) As String
Dim num As Integer
Private Sub addName ()

```
For num = 1 To 10
studentName (num) = InputBox ("Enter the student name", "Enter
Name", "", 1500, 4500)
If studentName (num) <> "" Then
Form1.Print studentName (num)
Else
End
End If
Next
End Sub

Private Sub Start_Click ()
Form1.Cls
addName
End Sub
```

The above program accepts data entries through an input box and displays the entries in the form itself. As you can see, this program will only allow a user to enter 10 names each time he clicks on the start button.

Example 17.2

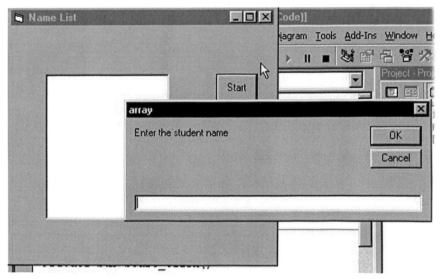

Figure 17.2

```
Dim studentName (10) As String
Dim num As Integer
Private Sub addName ( )
For num = 1 To 10
studentName (num) = InputBox ("Enter the student name")
List1.AddItem studentName (num)
Next
End Sub
Private Sub Start_Click ()
addName
End Sub
```

The above program accepts data entries through an InputBox and displays the items in a list box.

17.3 The Control Array

Sometimes we need a group of controls that are of the same type or perform similar tasks, for example the buttons on a calculator or a group of images boxes. Then we have to create an array of the controls. These controls will carry the same name but with different suffixes or indices.

It is very easy to create a control array in Visual Basic. Let's say you want to create a control array of a group of image boxes. The first step is to insert an image box in the form. Secondly, right-click on the image box, then click copy and paste. Visual Basic will ask you whether you want to create a control array or not. Click Yes to create a control array. Otherwise, another individual image box will be created. You can keep on clicking the paste button to obtain the number of controls you desire.

For example, a control array of a group of image boxes will comprise of Image1 (0), Image1 (1), Image1 (2), Image1 (3) and so on, which can be identified by their index values (or the values of the suffixes).

Exercise 17
1. Write a program to enter the item number and item unit price of 20 products using an input box.
2. Create an array of 6 shape controls and display them as different shapes.

Lesson 18

Arrays Part II -Two Dimensional Arrays

- Understanding the concept of a two dimensional array.
- Learning how to create a two dimensional array.

Multidimensional arrays are often needed when we are dealing with more complex programs, especially those that handle large amount of data. Data are usually organized and arranged in table form, this is where the multidimensional array comes into play. However, we are dealing only with two dimensional arrays, i.e. a table that consists of rows and columns.

The format to declare a two dimensional array is
Dim arrayName (num1, num2) as datatype
where num1 is the suffix of the first dimension of the last element and num2 is the suffix of the second dimension of the last element in the array. The suffixes of the element in the array will start with (0, 0) unless you set the Option Base to 1. In the case when the Option Base is set to 1, then the suffixes of the element in the array will start with (1, 1). For example,
Dim Score (5, 5) as Integer
will create a two dimension array consists of 36 elements. These elements can be organized in a table form as shown in Table 18.1:

Score(0,0)	Score(0,1)	Score(0,2)	Score(0,3)	Score(0,4)	Score(0,5)
Score(1,0)	Score(1,1)	Score(1,2)	Score(1,3)	Score(1,4)	Score(1,5)
Score(2,0)	Score(2,1)	Score(2,2)	Score(2,3)	Score(2,4)	Score(2,5)
Score(3,0)	Score(3,1)	Score(3,2)	Score(3,3)	Score(3,4)	Score(3,5)
Score(4,0)	Score(4,1)	Score(4,2)	Score(4,3)	Score(4,4)	Score(4,5)
Score(5,0)	Score(5,1)	Score(5,2)	Score(5,3)	Score(5,4)	Score(5,5)

Table 18.1 A two dimensional array

If you set the Option Base to 1, then the elements will start with (1,1) and end at (6,6) as shown in the following example.

Dim Score (6, 6) as Integer
Option Base 1

Score(1,1)	Score(1,2)	Score(1,3)	Score(1,4)	Score(1,5)	Score(1,6
Score(2,1)	Score(2,2)	Score(2,3)	Score(2,4)	Score(2,5)	Score(2,6)
Score(3,1)	Score(3,2)	Score(3,3)	Score(3,4	Score(3,5)	Score(3,6)
Score(4,1)	Score(4,2)	Score(4,3)	Score(4,4)	Score(4,5)	Score(4,6)
Score(5,1)	Score(5,2)	Score(5,3)	Score(5,4)	Score(5,5)	Score(5,6)
Score(6,1)	Score(6,2)	Score(6,3)	Score(6,4)	Score(6,5)	Score(6,6)

Table 18.2 A two dimensional array with Option Base 1

The above concepts are illustrated in a sample program in Example 18.1:

Example 18.1

```
Option Base 1
Dim score (6, 6) As Integer
Dim x As Integer
Dim sum As Integer

Private Sub Command1_Click ()
x = 0
For i = 1 To 6
For j = 1 To 6
sum = i + j
score (i, j) = sum
Label1(x).Caption = "Score (" & i & "," & j & ")" & "=" & sum
x = x + 1
Next j
Next i
End Sub
```

In Example 18.1, a two dimensional array that comprises 36 elements is created as the Option Base is set to 1. In order to display the elements, a nested For...Next loop is used to assign values which are equal to the sums of the suffixes, i and j, to all of the elements in the array. The values are displayed through a control array made up of 36 labels. The index is initially assigned a value of 0 using the variable x, which then increases by 1 after every loop. In this way the indices will be assigned the values ranging from 0 to 35, hence every label will be able to display the corresponding scores of the two dimensional array using the statement (the ampersand sign '&' is used to combine string and numeric data, and it is very useful for presenting an output that is easy to understand): **Label1(x).Caption = "Score (" & i & "," & j & ")" & "=" & sum**

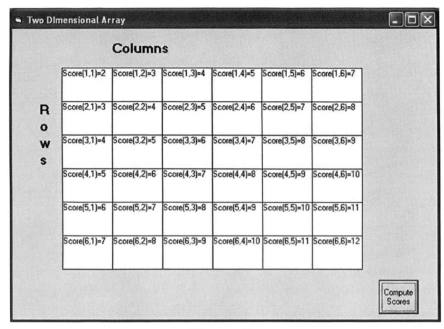

Figure 18.1

Exercise 18

1.   Write a program using a two-dimensional array to display the quarterly sales target achieved by 10 salesmen in a year. The sample output is shown below:

	Quarter 1	Quarter 2	Quarter 3	Quarter 4
Abraham	100	150	200	180
Ben	50	80	90	100
Chris	150	100	170	200
Dan	200	100	150	190
Elvis	80	80	90	100
Francis	90	70	50	80
Graham	110	120	130	160
Hans	160	170	180	190
Irwin	130	140	150	140
Jenkin	90	80	60	70

2. Write a program to input the marks of five subjects for 10 students and compute the total and average marks.

Lesson 19

Graphics

- Learning how to manipulate the line and shape controls.
- Learning how to use the image box and the picture box.
- Learning how to use PSet, Line and Circle Drawing methods.
- Learning how to create a picture viewer.

Graphics are a very important part of Visual Basic programming as an attractive interface will be appealing to the users. In old BASIC, drawing and designing graphics are considered as difficult jobs, as they have to be programmed line by line in a text-based environment. However, in Visual Basic, these jobs have been made easy. There are four basic controls in Visual Basic that you can use to draw graphics on your form: the line control, the shape control, the image box and the picture box.

19.1 The line and Shape controls

To draw a straight line, just click on the line control and then use your mouse to draw the line on the form. After drawing the line, you can then change its color, width and style using the BorderColor, BorderWidth and BorderStyle properties.

Similarly, to draw a shape, just click on the shape control and draw the shape on the form. The default shape is a rectangle, with the shape property set at 0. You can change the shape to square, oval, circle and rounded rectangle by changing the shape property's value to 1, 2, 3, 4, and 5 respectively. In addition, you can change its background color using the BackColor property, its border style using the BorderStyle property, its border color using the BorderColor property as well its border width using the BorderWidth property.

Example 19.1

The program in this example allows the user to change the shape by selecting a particular shape from a list of options from a list box, as well as changing its color through a common dialog box.

The objects to be inserted in the form are a list box, a command button, a shape control and a common dialog box. The common dialog box can be inserted by clicking on 'project' on the menu and then selecting the Microsoft Common Dialog Control 6.0 by clicking the check box. After that, the Microsoft Common Dialog Control 6.0 will appear in the toolbox and you can drag it into the form.

The list of items can be added to the list box through the AddItem method. The procedure for the common dialog box to present the standard colors is as follows:

CommonDialog1.Flags = &H1&
CommonDialog1.ShowColor
Shape1.BackColor = CommonDialog1.Color

The last line will change the background color of the shape by clicking on a particular color on the common dialog box as shown in Figure 19.2.

```
Private Sub Form_Load ()
List1.AddItem "Rectangle"
List1.AddItem "Square"
List1.AddItem "Oval"
List1.AddItem "Circle"
List1.AddItem "Rounded Rectangle"
List1.AddItem "Rounded Square"
End Sub

Private Sub List1_Click ()
Select Case List1.ListIndex
Case 0
Shape1.Shape = 0
Case 1
Shape1.Shape = 1
Case 2
```

```
Shape1.Shape = 2
Case 3
Shape1.Shape = 3
Case 4
Shape1.Shape = 4
Case 5
Shape1.Shape = 5
End Select
End Sub

Private Sub Command1_Click()
CommonDialog1.Flags = &H1&
CommonDialog1.ShowColor
Shape1.BackColor = CommonDialog1.Color
End Sub
```

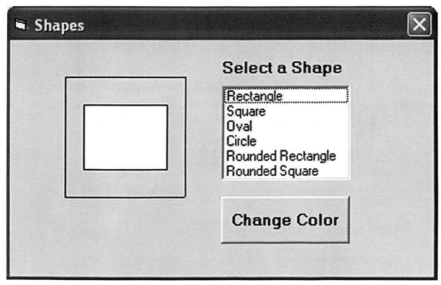

Figure 19.1 The output of Example 19.1

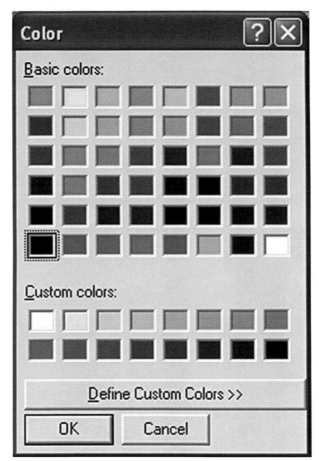

Figure 19.2 The Standard Colors

19.2 The Image Box and the Picture Box

Using the line and shape controls to draw graphics will only enable you to create a simple design. In order to improve the look of the interface, you need to put in images and pictures of your own. Fortunately, there are two very useful graphics tools you can use in Visual Basic which are the image box and the picture box.

To load a picture or image into an image box or a picture box, you can click on the picture property in the properties window and a dialog box will appear which will prompt the user to select a certain picture file. You can also load a picture at runtime by using the **LoadPicture ( )** method. The syntax is

Image1.Picture= LoadPicture ("C:\path name\picture file name")

or

picture1.Picture= LoadPicture ("C:\path name\picture name")

For example, the following statement will load the grape.gif picture into the image box.

Image1.Picture= LoadPicture ("C:\My Folder\Visual Basic program\Images\grape.gif")

Example 19.2

In this example, each time you click on the 'change pictures' button as shown in Figure 19.3, you will be able to see three images loaded into the image boxes. This program uses the Rnd function to generate random integers and then uses the LoadPicture method to load different pictures into the image boxes using the If...Then...Statements based on the random numbers generated. The output is shown in Figure 19.3.

```
Dim a, b, c As Integer
Private Sub Command1_Click ()
Randomize Timer
a = 3 + Int (Rnd * 3)
b = 3 + Int (Rnd * 3)
c = 3 + Int (Rnd * 3)

If a = 3 Then
Image1 (0).Picture = LoadPicture ("C:\My Folder\Visual Basic
program\Images\grape.gif")
End If
If a = 4 Then
Image1 (0).Picture = LoadPicture ("C:\My Folder\Visual Basic
program\Images\cherry.gif")
End If
If a = 5 Then
Image1 (0).Picture = LoadPicture ("C:\My Folder\Visual Basic
program\Images\orange.gif")
End If
If b = 3 Then
```

```
    Image1 (1).Picture = LoadPicture ("C:\My Folder\Visual Basic
program\Images\grape.gif")
    End If
    If b = 4 Then
    Image1 (1).Picture = LoadPicture ("C:\My Folder\Visual Basic
program\Images\cherry.gif")
    End If
    If b = 5 Then
    Image1 (1).Picture = LoadPicture ("C:\My Folder\Visual Basic
program\Images\orange.gif")
    End If
    If c = 3 Then
    Image1 (2).Picture = LoadPicture ("C:\My Folder\Visual Basic
program\Images\grape.gif")
    End If
    If c = 4 Then
    Image1 (2).Picture = LoadPicture ("C:\My Folder\Visual Basic
program\Images\cherry.gif")
    End If
    If c = 5 Then
    Image1 (2).Picture = LoadPicture ("C:\My Folder\Visual Basic
program\Images\orange.gif")
    End If
    End Sub
```

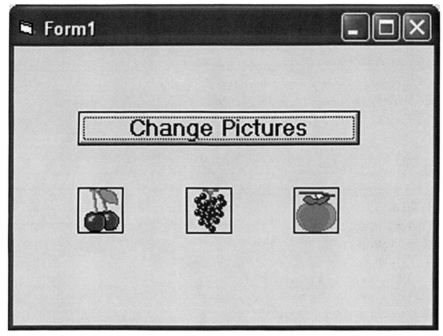

Figure 19.3

19.3 PSet, Line and Circle Drawing Methods

Other than using the line and shape controls to draw graphics on the form, you can also use the Pset, Line and Circle methods.

(a) The Pset Method

The Pset method draws a dot on the screen. The format is
Pset (x, y), color
(x,y) is the coordinates of the point and color is its color. To specify the color, you can use the color codes or the standard Visual Basic color constant such as VbRed, VbBlue, VbGeen etc. For example, Pset (100,200), VbRed will display a red dot at the (100,200) coordinates.

The Pset method can also be used to draw a straight line on the form. The procedure is
For x= a to b

Pset(x, x)
Next x

This procedure will draw a line starting from the point (a, a) and to the point (b, b). For example, the following procedure will draw a magenta line from the point (0, 0) to the point (1000, 1000).

For x= 0 to 100
Pset(x, x), vbMagenta
Next x

(b) The Line Method

Although the Pset method can be used to draw a straight line on the form, it is a little slow. It is better to use the Line method if you want to draw a straight line faster. The format of the Line command is shown below. It draws a line from the point (x1, y1) to the point (x2, y2) and the color constant will determine the color of the line.

Line (x1, y1)-(x2, y2), color

For example, the following command will draw a red line from the point (0, 0) to the point (1000, 2000).

Line (0, 0)-(1000, 2000), VbRed

The Line method can also be used to draw a rectangle. The format is

Line (x1-y1)-(x2, y2), color, B

The four corners of the rectangle are **(x1-y1), (x2-y1), (x1-y2)** and **(x2, y2)**

Another variation of the Line method is to fill the rectangle with a certain color. The format is

Line (x1, y1)-(x2, y2), color, BF

If you wish to draw the graphics in a picture box, you can use the following formats

- Picture1.Line (x1, y1)-(x2, y2), color
  - Picture1.Line (x1-y1)-(x2, y2), color, B
  - Picture1.Line (x1-y1)-(x2, y2), color, BF
- Picture1.Circle (x1, y1), radius, color

(c) The Circle Method

The circle method takes the following format

Circle (x1, y1), radius, color

This draws a circle centered at (x1, y1), with a certain radius and a certain border color. For example, the procedure

Circle (400, 400), 500, VbRed
draws a circle centered at (400, 400) with a radius of 500 twips and
a red border.

Example 19.3
This example is a program that can draw various shapes with
different colors in a picture box. The program uses a common dialog
box to select the color for the graphics. The output is shown in Figure
19.4.

```
Dim x1 As Integer
Dim y1 As Integer
Dim x2 As Integer
Dim y2 As Integer
Dim x3 As Integer
Dim y3 As Integer
Dim color As String
Dim r As Integer

Private Sub Command1_Click ()
On Error GoTo AddCoordinate
x1 = Text1.Text
y1 = Text2.Text
x2 = Text3.Text
y2 = Text4.Text
On Error GoTo addcolor
Picture1.Line (x1, y1)-(x2, y2), color
Exit Sub
AddCoordinate:
MsgBox ("Please fill in the coordinates")
Exit Sub
addcolor:
MsgBox ("Please choose a color")
Exit Sub
End Sub
Private Sub Command2_Click ()
x1 = Text1.Text
y1 = Text2.Text
x2 = Text3.Text
y2 = Text4.Text
```

```
Picture1.Line (x1, y1)-(x2, y2), color, B
End Sub

Private Sub Command3_Click ()
CommonDialog1.Flags = &H1&
CommonDialog1.ShowColor
color = CommonDialog1.color
End Sub

Private Sub Command4_Click ()
On Error GoTo addvalues
x3 = Text5.Text
y3 = Text6.Text
r = Text7.Text
Picture1.Circle (x3, y3), r, color
Exit Sub
addvalues:
MsgBox ("Please fill in the coordinates, the radius and the color")
End Sub

Private Sub Command5_Click ()
Picture1.Cls
End Sub
Private Sub Command6_Click ()
x1 = Text1.Text
y1 = Text2.Text
x2 = Text3.Text
y2 = Text4.Text
Picture1.Line (x1, y1)-(x2, y2), color, BF
End Sub
```

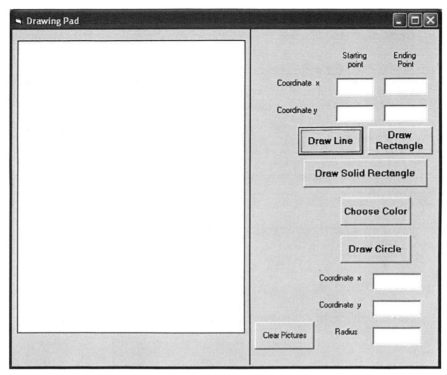

Figure 19.4

Example 19.4 The Picture Viewer

Let's create a program that enables the users to open and choose files from the folders in their PC. This can be done easily using a picture box and a common dialog box. In this program, you need to insert a picture box, a common dialog box and an image. In the image properties windows, click on the picture property and select a picture that resembles an open file icon. The procedure to open the common dialog box to browse the picture files as well as to load the selected picture into the picture box is CommonDialog1.Filter = "Bitmaps (*.BMP)|*.BMP|Metafiles (*.WMF)|*.WMF|Jpeg Files (*.jpg)|*.jpg|GIF Files (*.gif)|*.gif|Icon Files (*.ico)|*.ico|All Files (*.*)|*.*"

CommonDialog1.ShowOpen

Picture1.Picture = LoadPicture (CommonDialog1.FileName)

The filter property of the common dialog box uses the format as shown below

Bitmaps (*.BMP)|*.BMP

to specify the file type, and uses the pipe line | to separate different file types.

Visual Basic supports most of the picture formats namely bmp, wmf, jpg, gif, ico (icon) and cur (cursor) files. The command

CommonDialog1.ShowOpen

is to open the common dialog box and the command

Picture1.Picture = LoadPicture (CommonDialog1.FileName)

is to load the selected picture file into the picture box.

The whole program is shown below and the output is shown in Figure 19.5.

```
Private Sub Image1_Click ()
CommonDialog1.Filter = "Bitmaps    (*.BMP)|*.BMP|Metafiles
(*.WMF)|*.WMF|Jpeg Files (*.jpg)|*.jpg|GIF Files (*.gif)|*.gif|Icon Files
(*.ico)|*.ico|All Files (*.*)|*.*"
CommonDialog1.ShowOpen
Picture1.Picture = LoadPicture (CommonDialog1.FileName)
End Sub
```

Figure 19.5: The Picture Viewer

Example 19.5 An Advanced Picture Viewer

We will create a picture viewer in such a way that it can search for all types of graphics in your drives and display them.

Similar to the previous project, in this project, you need to insert a ComboBox, a DriveListBox, a DirListBox, a TextBox and a FileListBox into your form. I shall briefly explain again the function of each of the above controls.

a) ComboBox

The ComboBox displays and enables the selection of different types of files.

b) DriveListBox

The DriveListBox allows the selection of different drives available in your PC.

c) DirListBox

The DirListBox displays the directories of a selected drive in your PC.

d) TextBox

The TextBox displays the selected files.

e) FileListBox

The FileListBox displays files that are available

Relevant codes must be written to coordinate all the above controls so that the application can work properly. The program should flow in the following logical way:

Step 1: User chooses the type of files he wants to display.

Step2: User selects the drive that might contain the relevant graphic files.

Step 3: User looks into directories and subdirectories for the files specified in step1. The files should be displayed in the FileListBox.

Step 4: User selects the files from the FileListBox and click the Show button.

Step 5: User clicks on the Exit button to end the application.

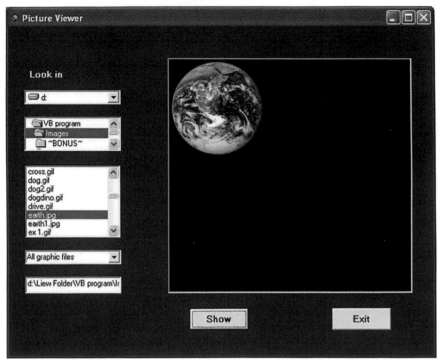

Figure 19.6: The Picture Viewer Interface

The Code

```
Private Sub Form_Load ()
Left = (Screen. Width—Width) \ 2
Top = (Screen. Height—Height) \ 2
Combo1.Text = "All graphic files"
Combo1.AddItem "All graphic files"
Combo1.AddItem "All files"
End Sub

Private Sub Combo1_Change ()
If ListIndex = 0 Then
File1.Pattern = ("*.bmp;*.wmf;*.jpg;*.gif")
Else
File1.Pattern = ("*.*")
End If
End Sub
```

```
Private Sub Dir1_Change ()
File1.Path = Dir1.Path
File1.Pattern = ("*.bmp;*.wmf;*.jpg;*.gif")
End Sub


Private Sub Drive1_Change ()
Dir1.Path = Drive1.Drive
End Sub


Private Sub File1_Click ()
If Combo1.ListIndex = 0 Then
File1.Pattern = ("*.bmp;*.wmf;*.jpg;*.gif")
Else
File1.Pattern = ("*.*")
End If

If Right (File1.Path, 1) <> "\" Then
filenam = File1.Path + "\" + File1.FileName
Else
filenam = File1.Path + File1.FileName
End If
Text1.Text = filenam
End Sub


Private Sub show_Click ()
If Right (File1.Path, 1) <> "\" Then
filenam = File1.Path + "\" + File1.FileName
Else
filenam = File1.Path + File1.FileName
End If
picture1.Picture = LoadPicture (filenam)
End Sub
```

Exercise 19
1. Write down the formats of the Pset method, the Line method and the Circle method.
2. Write a program to draw a circle which color can be changed using the colors specified in a list box.

3. Write a program to load pictures of various formats into an image box using the common dialog box.

4. Write a program that can load a set of pictures randomly into a picture box.

Lesson 20

Creating Multimedia Applications

- Learning how to create a CD player.
- Learning how to create an Audio player.
- Learning how to create a Multimedia player.

In Visual Basic, you can create various multimedia applications that can play audio CD, various audio files including mp3, wav and midi files, and different types of video files such as avi, mpeg files and etc. To be able to play multimedia files or multimedia devices, you have to insert the Microsoft Multimedia Control into your Visual Basic applications that you are going to create. However, Microsoft Multimedia Control is not normally included in the startup toolbox. Therefore, you need to add the Microsoft Multimedia control by pressing Ctrl+T and checking the box beside the Microsoft Multimedia control 6.0 from the components that are displayed in the dialog box as shown in Figure 20.1. Then, press the OK button. When you close the dialog box, you will notice that the Microsoft Multimedia Control will be available in the toolbox and you can drag it into the form.

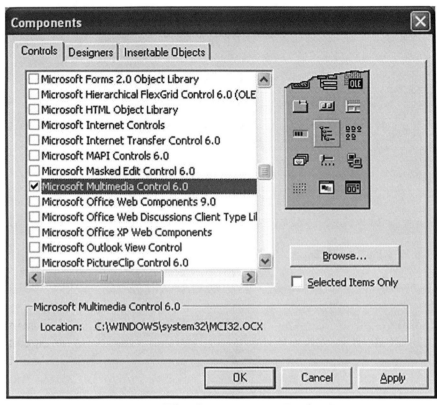

Figure 20.1 The Components Dialog Box

20.1 Creating a CD Player

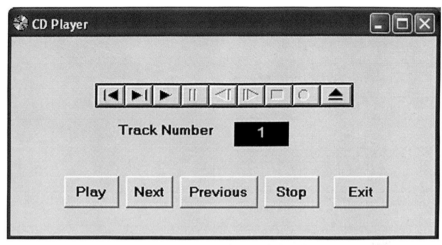

Figure 20.2: The Interface of the CD player

In this program, you will insert the Microsoft Multimedia Control and set its properties to Visible: True as well as Play: Enabled. In addition, insert five command buttons and name as well as label them as Play, Next, Previous, Stop and Exit. Besides that, insert a label that can be used to display the current track number of the song being played. Lastly, enter the program codes.

The most important statement in this program is to set the Microsoft Multimedia Control's device type to CDAudio because it will ensure audio CDs can be played.

MMControl1.DeviceType = "CDAudio"

To display the track number of the current song being played, use the following statement:

trackNum.Caption = MMControl1.Track

The Play, Next, Previous and Stop commands can be programmed using the

MMControl1.Command = "Play", MMControl1.Command = "Next", MMControl1.Command = "Prev", and MMControl1.Command = "Stop" statement.

Lastly, always ensure that the Microsoft Multimedia Control is closed whenever the user closes the player. This can be achieved by using the statement

MMControl1.Command = "Close"

Under Form1_Unload procedure.

The program:

```
Private Sub Form_Load ()
'To position the page at the center
Left = (Screen.Width—Width) \ 2
Top = (Screen.Height—Height) \ 2
End Sub

Private Sub Form_Activate ()
'Load the CDPlayer
MMControl1.Notify = False
MMControl1.Wait = True
MMControl1.DeviceType = "CDAudio"
MMControl1.Command = "Open"
End Sub

Private Sub MMControl1_StatusUpdate ()
'Update the track number
trackNum.Caption = MMControl1.Track
End Sub

Private Sub Next_Click ()
MMControl1.Command = "Next"
End Sub

Private Sub Play_Click ()
MMControl1.Command = "Play"
End Sub

Private Sub Previous_Click ()
MMControl1.Command = "Prev"
End Sub

Private Sub Stop_Click ()
MMControl1.Command = "Stop"
End Sub

Private Sub Exit_Click ()
MMControl1.Command = "Stop"
MMControl1.Command = "Close"
```

```
End
End Sub

Private Sub Form1_unload ()
'Unload the CDPlayer
MMControl1.Command = "Close"
End Sub
```

20.2 Creating an Audio Player

In section 20.1, we have programmed a CD player. Now, with some minor modifications, we will transform the CD player into an audio player. This player will be created in such a way that it can search for wave and midi files in your drives and play them. In this project, you need to insert a ComboBox, a DriveListBox, a DirListBox, a TextBox and a FileListBox into your form. I shall briefly discuss the function of each of the above controls. Besides that, you must also insert Microsoft Multimedia Control (MMControl) in your form. You may make it visible or invisible. In this program, I choose to make it invisible so that I can use the command buttons created to control the player. The functions of the various controls are explained below:

a) The ComboBox

Displays and enables the selection of different types of files. To add items to the Combo Box, you can use the AddItem method. The items here are the extensions of different audio files.

b) The DriveListBox

The DriveListBox allows the selection of different drives in your computer.

c) The DirListBox

The DirListBox displays different directories that are available in your computer.

d) The Textbox

The Textbox displays the selected files.

e) The FileListBox

The FileListBox displays files that are available in your computer.

Relevant codes must be written to coordinate all the above controls so that the application can work properly. The program should flow in the following logical steps:

Step 1: User chooses the type of files he wants to play.

Step2: User selects the drive that might contain the relevant audio files.

Step 3: User looks into directories and subdirectories for the files specified in step1. The files should be displayed in the FileListBox.

Step 4: User selects the files from the FileListBox and clicks the Play button.

Step 5: User clicks on the Stop button to stop playing and the Exit button to end the application.

To coordinate the DriveListBox and the DirListBox, you can use the statement below, so that any change of the drives will be reflected in the directory list box.

Dir1.Path = Drive1.Drive

To coordinate the FileListBox and the DirListBox, you can use the statement below so that any change of the directories will be reflected in the File List Box.

File1.Path = Dir1.Path

To select the target file, you can use the following statements where File1.Path determines the path of the file and File1.FileName determines the file name. The file name is then assigned to the variable filename and displayed in the text box.

```
If Right (File1.Path, 1) <> "\" Then
filenam = File1.Path + "\" + File1.FileName
Else
filenam = File1.Path + File1.FileName
End If
Text1.Text = filenam
```

To select the file types, you can use the statement File1.Pattern = ("*.wav") to choose the wave audio files and the statement File1.Pattern = ("*.mid") to choose the sequencer files.

To play the selected file, use the following procedure:

```
Private Sub play_Click ()
'To play WaveAudio file or Midi File
If Combo1.ListIndex = 0 Then
MMControl1.DeviceType = "WaveAudio"
ElseIf Combo1.ListIndex = 1 Then
MMControl1.DeviceType = "Sequencer"
End If
MMControl1.FileName = Text1.Text
MMControl1.Command = "Open"
MMControl1.Command = "Play"
End Sub
```

The statement **MMControl1.DeviceType = "WaveAudio"** enables the Microsoft Multimedia Control to play Wave Audio files and the statement **MMControl1.DeviceType = "Sequencer"** enables the Microsoft Multimedia Control to play the midi files. In fact, the Microsoft Multimedia Control can play many other types of multimedia files, including Mpeg, Mp3 and Avi video files.

The statement **MMControl1.FileName = Text1.Text** plays the multimedia file displayed in the Text1 textbox. The statement **MMControl1.Command = "Open"** initiates the Microsoft Multimedia Control and the statement **MMControl1.Command = "Play"** plays the multimedia file. The statement **MMControl1.Command = "stop"** stops the Microsoft Multimedia Control from playing and finally the statement **MMControl1.Command = "Close"** closes the Microsoft Multimedia Control.

The Program

```
Private Sub Form_Load ()
'To center the Audioplayer
Left = (Screen.Width—Width) \ 2
Top = (Screen.Height—Height) \ 2
Combo1.Text = "*.wav"
Combo1.AddItem "*.wav"
Combo1.AddItem "*.mid"
Combo1.AddItem "All files"
End Sub
```

```
Private Sub Combo1_Change ()
'To determine file type
If ListIndex = 0 Then
File1.Pattern = ("*.wav")
ElseIf ListIndex = 1 Then
File1.Pattern = ("*.mid")
Else
Fiel1.Pattern = ("*.*")
End If
End Sub


Private Sub Dir1_Change ()
'To change directories and subdirectories (or folders and
subfolders)
File1.Path = Dir1.Path
If Combo1.ListIndex = 0 Then
File1.Pattern = ("*.wav")
ElseIf Combo1.ListIndex = 1 Then
File1.Pattern = ("*.mid")
Else
File1.Pattern = ("*.*")
End If
End Sub


Private Sub Drive1_Change ()
'To change drives
Dir1.Path = Drive1.Drive
End Sub


Private Sub File1_Click ()
If Combo1.ListIndex = 0 Then
File1.Pattern = ("*.wav")
ElseIf Combo1.ListIndex = 1 Then
File1.Pattern = ("*.mid")
Else
File1.Pattern = ("*.*")
End If
If Right(File1.Path, 1) <> "\" Then
filenam = File1.Path + "\" + File1.FileName
Else
filenam = File1.Path + File1.FileName
End If
Text1.Text = filenam
```

```
End Sub
Private Sub play_Click ()
'To play WaveAudio file or Midi file
If Combo1.ListIndex = 0 Then
MMControl1.DeviceType = "WaveAudio"
ElseIf Combo1.ListIndex = 1 Then
MMControl1.DeviceType = "Sequencer"
End If
MMControl1.FileName = Text1.Text
MMControl1.Command = "Open"
MMControl1.Command = "Play"
End Sub
Private Sub stop_Click ()
MMControl1.Command = "Stop"
End Sub

Private Sub Exit_Click ()
MMControl1.Command = "Close"
End
End Sub
```

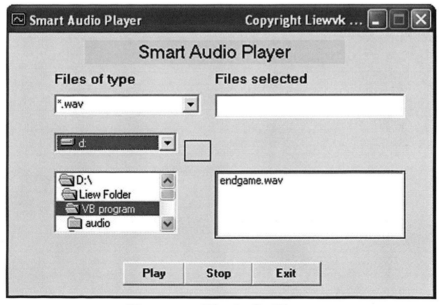

Figure 20.3 The Audio Player

20.3 Creating a Multimedia Player

In section 20.2, we have created an audio player. Now, with further modifications, we will transform the audio player into a multimedia player that can play all kinds of movie files besides audio files. This player will be created in such a way that it can search for all types of media files in your computer drives and play them.

In this project, you need to insert a ComboBox, a DriveListBox, a DirListBox, a TextBox, a FileListBox, and a picture box (for playing movies) into your form. I shall briefly discuss the function of each of the above controls. You must also insert Microsoft Multimedia Control (MMControl) in your form; you may make it visible or invisible. In my program, I choose to make it invisible so that I can use the command buttons created to control the player.

The program is almost similar to the audio player, but you need to add a few extra statements so that you can play the video files and also the mp3 files. First of all, you have to add two more file types with the statements **File1.Pattern = ("*.avi")** and **File1.Pattern = ("*. mpeg;*.mpg;*.mp3")** so that the Avi and Mpeg movie files as well as the mp3 files will show up in the file list box . Secondly, you have to add the statement **MMControl1.DeviceType = "AVIVideo"** so that the Microsoft Multimedia Control can play the Avi video files and **MMControl1.DeviceType = " "** so that the player can play other media files including the mp3 files.

Figure 20.4: The Multimedia Player

The Program

```
Private Sub Form_Load ()
Left = (Screen.Width—Width) \ 2
Top = (Screen.Height—Height) \ 2
Combo1.Text = "*.wav"
Combo1.AddItem "*.wav"
Combo1.AddItem "*.mid"
Combo1.AddItem "*.avi"
Combo1.AddItem "*.mpeg;*.mpg;*.mp3"
Combo1.AddItem "All files"
End Sub

Private Sub Combo1_Change ()
If ListIndex = 0 Then
File1.Pattern = ("*.wav")
ElseIf ListIndex = 1 Then
File1.Pattern = ("*.mid")
```

```
ElseIf ListIndex = 2 Then
File1.Pattern = ("*.avi")
ElseIf ListIndex = 3 Then
File1.Pattern = ("*.mpeg;*.mpg;*.mp3")
Else
File1.Pattern = ("*.*")
End If
End Sub

Private Sub Dir1_Change ()
File1.Path = Dir1.Path
If Combo1.ListIndex = 0 Then
File1.Pattern = ("*.wav")
ElseIf Combo1.ListIndex = 1 Then
File1.Pattern = ("*.mid")
ElseIf Combo1.ListIndex = 2 Then
File1.Pattern = ("*.avi")
ElseIf Combo1.ListIndex = 3 Then
File1.Pattern = ("*.mpeg;*.mpg;*.mp3")
Else
File1.Pattern = ("*.*")
End If
End Sub

Private Sub Drive1_Change ()
Dir1.Path = Drive1.Drive
End Sub

Private Sub File1_Click ()
If Combo1.ListIndex = 0 Then
File1.Pattern = ("*.wav")
ElseIf Combo1.ListIndex = 1 Then
File1.Pattern = ("*.mid")
ElseIf Combo1.ListIndex = 2 Then
File1.Pattern = ("*.avi")
ElseIf Combo1.ListIndex = 3 Then
File1.Pattern = ("*.mpeg;*.mpg;*.mp3")
Else
File1.Pattern = ("*.*")
End If
If Right (File1.Path, 1) <> "\" Then
```

```
filenam = File1.Path + "\" + File1.FileName
Else
filenam = File1.Path + File1.FileName
End If
Text1.Text = filenam
End Sub


Private Sub Exit_Click ()
MMControl1.Command = "Close"
End
End Sub
Private Sub Open_Click ()
If Combo1.ListIndex = 0 Then
MMControl1.DeviceType = "WaveAudio"
End If
If Combo1.ListIndex = 1 Then
MMControl1.DeviceType = "Sequencer"
End If
If Combo1.ListIndex = 2 Then
MMControl1.DeviceType = "AVIVideo"
End If
If Combo1.ListIndex = 3 Then
MMControl1.DeviceType = ""
End If
MMControl1.FileName = Text1.Text
MMControl1.Command = "Open"
End Sub


Private Sub play_Click ()
Timer1.Enabled = True
MMControl1.Command = "Play"
MMControl1.hWndDisplay = Picture1.hWnd
End Sub


Private Sub stop_Click ()
If MMControl1.Mode = 524 Then Exit Sub
If MMControl1.Mode <> 525 Then
MMControl1.Wait = True
MMControl1.Command = "Stop"
End If
MMControl1.Wait = True
```

MMControl1.Command = "Close"
End Sub

Exercise 20

1. Write a program that can play different sound files using a common dialog box.
2. Write a program that can play different video files using a common dialog box.
3. Create a player that can play audio CDs as well as different sound files.

Lesson 21

Animation-Part I

- Learning how to create simple animation in Visual Basic.

Animation is always an interesting and exciting part of programming. Although Visual Basic is not designed to handle advanced animations, you can still create some interesting animated effects if you put in some hard thinking. There are many ways to create animated effects in Visual Basic 6, but for a start we will focus on the easier methods.

The simplest way to create animation is to set the visible property of a group of images or pictures or even texts and labels to true or false by triggering a set of events such as clicking a button. Let's examine the following example:

Example 21.1

This is a program that creates the illusion of moving a jet plane in four directions, that is, north, south, east, and west. In order to do this, we need to insert five images of the same picture into the form. Set the visible property of the image in the center to be true and set the rest to false. On start-up, the user will only be able to see the image in the center. Next, insert four command buttons into the form and change the labels to Move North, Move East, Move West and Move South respectively. Double click on the Move North button and key in the following procedure:

```
Sub Command1_click ()
Image1.Visible = False
Image3.Visible = True
Image2.Visible = False
Image4.Visible = False
Image5.Visible = False
End Sub.
```

By clicking on the Move North button, Image1 and other images except Image3 will be displayed. This will give an illusion that the jet plane has moved north. Now, double click on other command buttons and key in similar procedures. You can also insert an additional command button and label it as Reset and key in the following code:

Image1.Visible = True

Image3.Visible = False

Image2.Visible = False

Image4.Visible = False

Image5.Visible = False

Clicking on the reset button will make the image in the center visible again while other images become invisible, this will give the impression that the jet plane has moved back to the original position.

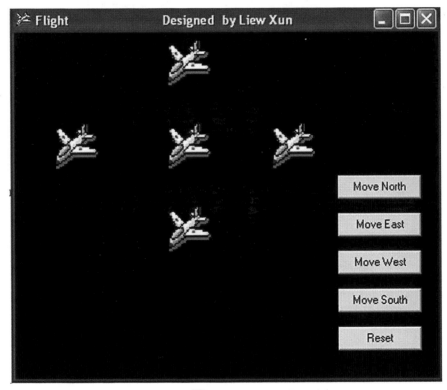

Figure 21.1

Example 21.1

You can also issue the commands using a textbox. This idea actually came from my son Xun (10). His program is shown below:

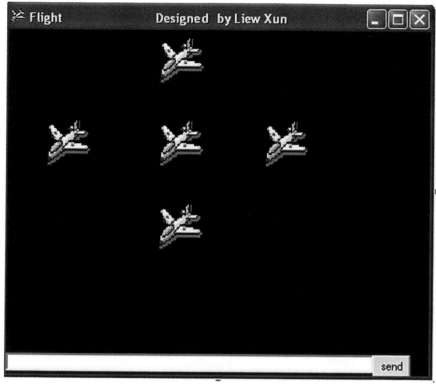

Figure 21.2

In the textbox, when you key in the letter n, the plane will move north, move west when you key in w, move south when you key in s and move east when you key in the letter e. The codes are as follows:

```
Private Sub Command1_Click()
If Text1.Text = "n" Then
Image1.Visible = False
Image3.Visible = True
Image2.Visible = False
Image4.Visible = False
Image5.Visible = False
ElseIf Text1.Text = "e" Then
Image1.Visible = False
Image4.Visible = True
Image2.Visible = False
Image3.Visible = False
Image5.Visible = False
```

```
ElseIf Text1.Text = "w" Then
Image1.Visible = False
Image3.Visible = False
Image2.Visible = False
Image4.Visible = False
Image5.Visible = True
ElseIf Text1.Text = "s" Then
Image1.Visible = False
Image3.Visible = False
Image2.Visible = True
Image4.Visible = False
Image5.Visible = False
End If
End Sub
```

Another simple way to simulate animation in Visual Basic6 is by using the Left and Top properties of an object. Image.Left gives the distance of the image in twips from the left border of the screen, and Image.Top gives the distance of the image in twips from the top border of the screen. 1 twip is equivalent to 1/1440 of an inch. Using a statement such as Image.Left-100 will move the Image100 twips to the left, Image.Left+100 will move the Image100 twip away from the left (or 100 twips to the right), Image.Top-100 will move the Image100 twips to the top and Image.Top+100 will move the Image100 twips away from the top border (or 100 twips down). Example 21.3 illustrates how all the above methods can be used to create animation.

Example 21.3

This is a program that can move an object up, down, left, and right every time you click on a relevant command button. The codes such as Image1.Top = Image1.Top + 100 are to make the distance increase or decrease every time a user clicks on the command button. For example, if the initial position of Image1 is 1000 twips from the top, after one click, the distance from the top will be 1100, and the next distance will be 1200 and so on. Therefore, by writing similar codes for all the four buttons, you can move the image in four directions by clicking any of the four buttons.

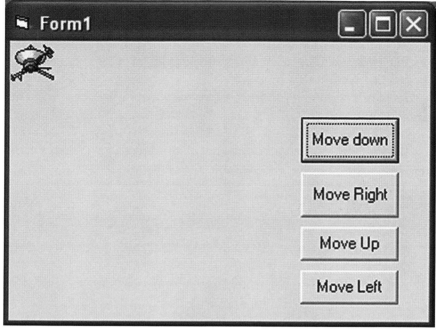

Figure 21.3

The Program

```
Private Sub Command1_Click ()
Image1.Top = Image1.Top + 100
End Sub

Private Sub Command2_Click ()
Image1.Top = Image1.Top—100
End Sub

Private Sub Command3_Click ()
Image1.Left = Image1.Left + 100
End Sub

Private Sub Command4_Click ()
Image1.Left = Image1.Left—100
End Sub
```

Example 21.4

This example lets users magnify or diminish an object by changing the height and width properties of an object. It is quite similar to the previous example. The statements Image1.Height = Image1.Height + 100 and Image1.Width = Image1.Width + 100 will increase the height and the width of an object by 100 twips each time a user clicks on the relevant command button. On the other hand, the statements Image1. Height = Image1.Height—100 and Image1.Width = Image1.Width -100 will decrease the height and the width of an object by 100 twips each time a user clicks on the relevant command button.

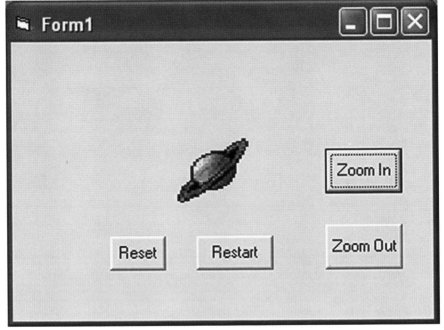

Figure 21.4

The Program

```
Private Sub Command1_Click ()
Image1.Height = Image1.Height + 100
Image1.Width = Image1.Width + 100
End Sub

Private Sub Command2_Click ()
Image1.Height = Image1.Height—100
```

```
Image1.Width = Image1.Width—100
End Sub
```

You can try to combine both of the programs and make an object move and increase or decrease in size each time a user clicks a command button.

Exercise 21

1. Create a simple animation by setting the visible property of a group of objects to false and true.
2. Create an animation program by varying an image's Left, Top, Width and Height properties.

Lesson 22

Animation — Part II

- Learning how to create a drag and drop animation.
- Learning how to create an animation with a complete motion.

22.1 Animation using a drag and drop procedure

Drag and drop is a common windows application where you can drag and drop an object such as a file into a folder or into a recycle bin. This ability can be easily programmed in Visual Basic. In the following example, you will create a jigsaw puzzle program using a drag and drop procedure.

In this program, you need to create nine images that are cut out from a single picture using a graphics program. Next, in the Visual Basic program, create a control array of eighteen images, from image1 (0) to image1 (17). The first nine image controls constitute of nine empty squares while the images that were created earlier will be loaded into the next nine image controls. When the user runs the program, he or she needs to drag the images into the correct squares. To be able to drag the images, the dragMode properties of the images that are to be dragged have to be set to 1(Automatic). Each image that is to be dragged needs to be identified using the tag property so that it can be put into the correct posiiton. In this program, the tags of the images are identified using the row and column concept, 11 means row 1 and column one, 21 means row 2 and column 1 and etc. Besides, you may load an appropriate icon under the dragIcon properties for those images to be dragged. Preferably the icon should be the same as the image so that when you drag the image, it is like you are dragging the image along.

Source refers to the image being dragged. Using the code Source. Visible=False means the image at the original position will disappear after being dragged into the correct position. The program uses the Source. Tag property to identify the correct image for a particular position. Besides, in order to identify the target square where an image is to be dropped, the program employs a Select Case..... End select procedure using index of the target image control as the selection criteria. The Select Case..... End select procedure is then put under the Private Sub Image1_DragDrop sub procedure.

The whole program is as follows:

```
Dim imgindex As Integer
Dim imgtag As String

Private Sub Image1_DragDrop(Index As Integer, Source As Control, X As Single, Y As Single)

imgtag = Source.Tag
imgindex = Index
Select Case imgindex

Case 0
If imgtag = 11 Then
Image1(0).Picture = Image1(9).Picture
Source.Visible = False
Else
Source.Visible = True
End If

Case 1
If imgtag = 12 Then
Image1(1).Picture = Image1(10).Picture
Source.Visible = False
Else
Source.Visible = True
End If

Case 2
If imgtag = 13 Then
Image1(2).Picture = Image1(11).Picture
Source.Visible = False
Else
```

```
Source.Visible = True
End If

Case 3
If imgtag = 21 Then
Image1(3).Picture = Image1(12).Picture
Source.Visible = False
Else
Source.Visible = True
End If

Case 4
If imgtag = 22 Then
Image1(4).Picture = Image1(13).Picture
Source.Visible = False
Else
Source.Visible = True
End If

Case 5
If imgtag = 23 Then
Image1(5).Picture = Image1(14).Picture
Source.Visible = False
Else
Source.Visible = True
End If

Case 6
If imgtag = 31 Then
Image1(6).Picture = Image1(15).Picture
Source.Visible = False
Else
Source.Visible = True
End If
Case 7
If imgtag = 32 Then
Image1(7).Picture = Image1(16).Picture
Source.Visible = False
Else
Source.Visible = True
End If
```

```
Case 8
If imgtag = 33 Then
Image1(8).Picture = Image1(17).Picture
Source.Visible = False
Else
Source.Visible = True
End If
End Select
End Sub
```

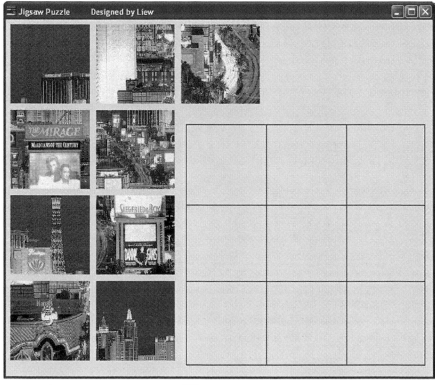

Figure 22.1

The Program

```
Private Sub Form_Click ()
Label1.Visible = False
End Sub
```

```
Private Sub Image4_DragDrop (Source As Control, X As Single, Y
As Single)
    Source.Visible = False
    If Source.Tag = "Fire" Then
    Image4.Picture = Image5.Picture
    End If
End Sub


Private Sub instruct_Click ()
    Label1.Visible = True
End Sub
```

22.2 Animation with complete motion

So far the examples of animation shown in Lesson 21 only involve movement of static images. In this Lesson, you will be able to create true animation where an action finishes in a complete cycle, for example, a butterfly flapping its wings. In the following example, you need to use eight picture frames of a butterfly which display a butterfly flapping its wings at different stages.

You need to put all the above images overlapping one another, make Image1 visible while all other images invisible at start-up. Next, insert a command button and label it as Animate. Click on the command button and key in the statements that make the images appear and disappear successively by using the properties image.visible=true and image.visible=false. You can use If..... Then and Elseif to control the program flow. When you run the program, you should be able to get the following animation.

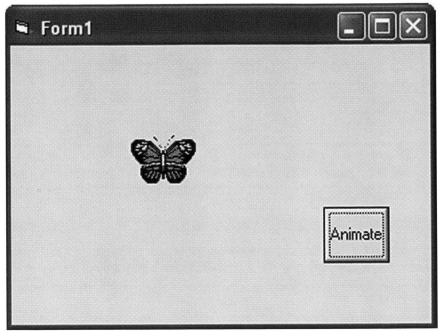

Figure 22.2

The Program

```
Private Sub Command1_Click ()
If Image1.Visible = True Then
Image1.Visible = False
Image2.Visible = True
ElseIf Image2.Visible = True Then
Image2.Visible = False
Image3.Visible = True
ElseIf Image3.Visible = True Then
Image3.Visible = False
Image4.Visible = True
ElseIf Image4.Visible = True Then
Image4.Visible = False
Image5.Visible = True
ElseIf Image5.Visible = True Then
Image5.Visible = False
Image6.Visible = True
ElseIf Image6.Visible = True Then
Image6.Visible = False
```

```
Image7.Visible = True
ElseIf Image7.Visible = True Then
Image7.Visible = False
Image8.Visible = True
ElseIf Image8.Visible = True Then
Image8.Visible = False
Image1.Visible = True
End If
End Sub
```

If you wish to create the effect of the butterfly flapping its wings and flying at the same time, then you could use the Left and Top properties of an object, such as the one used in the examples of Lesson 23. Below is an example of a subroutine where the butterfly will flap its wings and move up at the same time. You can also write subroutines that move the butterfly to the left, to the right and to the bottom.

```
Sub move_up ()
If Image1.Visible = True Then
Image1.Visible = False
Image2.Visible = True
Image2.Top = Image2.Top — 100
ElseIf Image2.Visible = True Then
Image2.Visible = False
Image3.Visible = True
Image3.Top = Image3.Top — 100
ElseIf Image3.Visible = True Then
Image3.Visible = False
Image4.Visible = True
Image4.Top = Image4.Top — 100
ElseIf Image4.Visible = True Then
Image4.Visible = False
Image5.Visible = True
Image5.Top = Image5.Top — 100
ElseIf Image5.Visible = True Then
Image5.Visible = False
Image6.Visible = True
Image6.Top = Image6.Top — 100
ElseIf Image6.Visible = True Then
Image6.Visible = False
Image7.Visible = True
Image7.Top = Image7.Top — 100
ElseIf Image7.Visible = True Then
```

```
Image7.Visible = False
Image8.Visible = True
Image8.Top = Image8.Top—100
ElseIf Image8.Visible = True Then
Image8.Visible = False
Image1.Visible = True
Image1.Top = Image1.Top—100
End If
End Sub
```

Exercise 22

1. Write a program that drags and drops a group of items into a box and plays a sound at the same time.

2. Create a program that simulates a running man using the images below or use your own images, or those downloaded from the Internet.

Lesson 23

Animation — Part III

- Learning how to create animation using timer.
- Learning how to create animation using the Move method.

23.1 Animation using timer

All preceding examples of animation that you have learnt in Lesson 21 and Lesson 22 only involve manual animation, which means you need to keep on clicking a certain command button or pressing a key to make an object animate. In order to make it move automatically, you need to use a timer. The first step in creating automatic animation is to drag the timer from the toolbox into the form and set its interval to a certain value other than 0. A value of 1 is equivalent to 1 milli-second which means a value of 1000 represents 1 second. The value of the timer interval will determine the speed of an animation.

Example 23.1

This program uses a very simple technique to create an animation by setting the properties Visible=False and Visible=True to show and hide two images alternately. When you click on the program, you should see the animation that shows Image1 and Image2 interchangeably.

The Program

```
Private Sub Timer1_Timer ()
If Image1.Visible = True Then
Image1.Visible = False
Image2.Visible = True
ElseIf Image2.Visible = True Then
Image2.Visible = False
Image1.Visible = True
End If
End Sub
```

Example 23.2

This example shows a complete cycle of a motion such as the butterfly flapping its wings. Previous examples show only manual animation while this example will display an automatic animation once you start the program or by clicking a command button. Similar to the example under Lesson 22.2, you need to insert a group of eight images of a butterfly flapping its wings at different stages. Next, insert a timer into the form and set the interval to 10 or any value you like. Remember to make Image1 visible and the other images invisible at start-up. Finally, insert a command button, rename its caption as Animate, and key in the following statements by double clicking on this button.

It is important to bear in mind that you should enter the statements for hiding and showing the images under the timer1_timer subroutine otherwise the animation will not work. Clicking on the Animate button will make the timer start ticking and the event will run after every interval of 10 milliseconds or whatever interval you have set.

Figure 23.1

The Program

```
Private Sub Form_Load ()
Image1.Visible = True
x = 0
End Sub

Private Sub Command1_Click ()
Timer1.Enabled = True
End Sub

Private Sub Timer1_Timer ()
If Image1.Visible = True Then
Image1.Visible = False
Image2.Visible = True

ElseIf Image2.Visible = True Then
Image2.Visible = False
Image3.Visible = True
ElseIf Image3.Visible = True Then
Image3.Visible = False
Image4.Visible = True
ElseIf Image4.Visible = True Then
Image4.Visible = False
Image5.Visible = True
ElseIf Image5.Visible = True Then
Image5.Visible = False
Image6.Visible = True
ElseIf Image6.Visible = True Then
Image6.Visible = False
Image7.Visible = True
ElseIf Image7.Visible = True Then
Image7.Visible = False
Image8.Visible = True
ElseIf Image8.Visible = True Then
Image8.Visible = False
Image1.Visible = True
End If
End Sub
```

23.2 Animation using the Move Method

The most powerful method to enable animation in Visual Basic is the Move method. The syntax to make the object move to the point (x,y) is shown below:

Object.Move x, y

where x is the distance from the left border of the screen and y is the distance from the top border of the screen. For example, the statement Image1.Move 1000, 1000 will move Image1 to the location 1000 twips from the left border and 1000 twips from the top border.

Example 23.3

This program will move Image1 to the location with coordinates (1000, 1000) at the first click and subsequently every click will move Image1 100 twips away from the left border and 100 twips from the top border.

```
Private Sub Image1_Click()
Image1.Move 1000 + x, 1000 + x
x = x + 100
End Sub
```

Example 23.4

This example uses the timer to initiate a motion that is automatic. In order to do that, you need to insert a timer and set its interval to a certain value. The procedure is shown below. When you run this program, the image moves 50 twips closer to the left and the top of the screen respectively after every interval.

```
Private Sub Image1_Click ()
Image1.Move Image1.Left-50, Image1.Top-50
End Sub
```

Exercise 23

1. Write down and explain the syntax of the Move method.
2. Create an animation that shows and hides a group of 5 images interchangeably.
3. Write a program using the Move method that shows an object moving vertically up and down.

Lesson 24

Fun and Games Programming –Part I

- Learning how to create simple games.

A lot of people might think that Visual Basic is not a suitable programming language for games. Actually, though there might be some limitations in Visual Basic involving game programming and animation, you can actually construct some good games in Visual Basic if you put in a lot of thought and time. To design a game, you need to come up with an idea first, and then sit back and think over it. Ideas can be obtained through the Internet, other media sources, from gamers themselves etc. After that, you need to write out a draft program and try it out. You should always start with one small component of the program and if that works, you can proceed to program other components and then combine them. You should always have a Visual Basic book in hand for referencing.

Game programming can be very satisfying if your programs work. Furthermore, you can learn a great deal of programming logics by doing game programming because the procedures are often very complex, and you need to look up for references every now and then.

Here are some of the programs that I have thought out myself. These programs make use of everything you have learnt so far and you need to read through all the procedures carefully so that you can better understand the programming logics behind them. Later, you might want to modify the programs or even come out with your own games.

24.1 Snake and Ladder Chess

Snake and Ladder chess is a popular board game for young children. This game usually involves two or more players and they take turns to move by rolling a die. On the way to the finishing point, the players will meet with some hurdles in the form of snakes and some opportunities in the form of ladders. Whenever the player encounters a snake (or more accurately, the snake's head), he or she will be thrown back to an earlier box (which is at the snake's tail). On the other hand, whenever the player encounters a ladder, he or she can climb up the ladder to a higher box. The player who reaches the finishing point first wins the game. Figure 24.1 illustrates the interface.

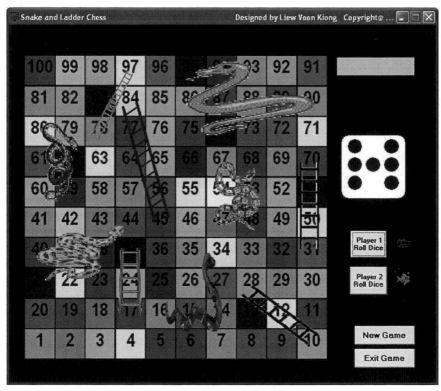

Figure 24.1 Snake and Ladder Chess

The first step in creating the game is to design the interface. Here, the labels used to design the chess board are numbered from 1 to 100. These labels are filled with different colors to give the chess board a more appealing look. Next, insert various pictures of snakes using the image box and then draw the ladders using the line tool. In addition, you need to draw the die with the shape control, and add in the command buttons for rolling the die, starting a new game as well as exiting the game. Besides that, you need to insert two images to denote the players and then put in the label for the declaration of the winner. Lastly, insert two timers for animation purposes.

The initial part of the program is to declare various variables. The two most important variables are the arrays c (10) and r (10). The array r (10) is used to denote the row numbers , where r(1)=row 1, r(2)=row 2 until r(10)=row 10. Similarly, c (10) is used to denote the column numbers, where c (1) =column 1, c (2) =column 2 until c (10) =column 10. After declaring the variables, you need to assign the coordinates of the center of all the boxes which can be denoted by (column, row) or (c (i), r (i)), using the procedure below:

```
Private Sub Form_Load ()
c (1) = 600
r(1) = 8200
For i = 1 To 9
c (i + 1) = c (i) + 800
Next
For j = 1 To 9
r (j + 1) = r (j) — 800
Next
End Sub
```

You have to determine the initial position of the center of the first box (label) by looking at its distance from the left as well as from the top, and also its width, in the properties window. In this program, the distance of the first box from the left is 400 twips, and its width is 800 twips, therefore its center is 600 twips from the left. Using the statement c (i + 1) = c (i) + 800 within a For...Next loop, the distance between successive columns will be fixed at 800 twips. Similarly, the distance between rows can be determined using the same logic.

The next most important step is to control the movement of the chess pieces. In order to do this, you have to use the variables totalnum and totalnum1 to denote the accumulated scores of the die for player 1 and player 2 respectively. For example, if the first score of the die is 3 and the second score of the die is 6 for player 1, then totalnum=9. You need to write the procedure for every row individually so that motion will be in a zigzag manner as shown in Figure 24.2

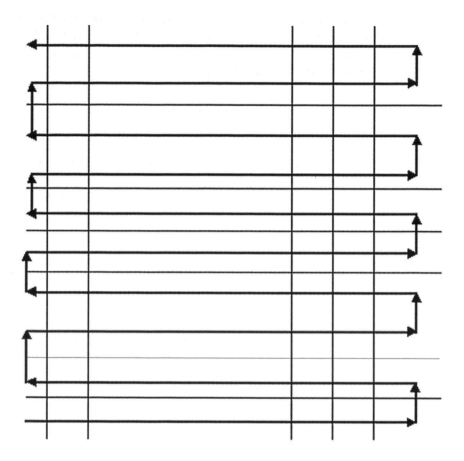

Figure 24.2 The movement of the chess pieces

For the first row and for player 1, you can use the following procedure:

```
If player = 1 Then
totalnum = totalnum + num
If totalnum < 11 Then
Image1 (0).Move c (totalnum), r (1)
End If
```

Num is the score which appears on the die and the totalnum is added to num to get the accumulated scores. In the first row, the number on the rightmost square is 10, which is equal to the number of columns across the first row. The statement

Image1 (0).Move c (totalnum), r (1) uses the Move method to move chess piece 1 (Image1(0)) across the column from left to right. For the movement in the second row, the direction is from right to left, so we need to use the following procedure:

If totalnum > 10 And totalnum < 21 Then
Image1 (0).Move c (21−totalnum), r (2)
End If
The statement Image1 (0).Move c(21−totalnum), r(2) will move Image1(0) from the position c(10),r(2) to c(1), r(2), i.e. from the square with number 11 to the square with number 20. The movement of the chess pieces for other positions follows the same logics. The procedure to move the chess pieces has to be placed under the Private Sub Timer1_ Timer procedure (set the Timer1's interval to a certain value).

Before the program can work, you will need to program the die, which will determine how many steps the chess pieces will move. The interface of the die consists of 7 round shapes that are placed in a rounded square as shown in Figure 24.1. The seven round shapes are inserted as a control array with names starting with shape1 (0) to shape1 (6). The shape in the center is shape1 (3). The appearance of the round shapes are controlled by a randomization process that produce six random numbers using the statement num = Int(1 + Rnd * 6). For example, when num=1, only the round shape in the center appears while other round shapes are made invisible. Other combinations use the same logic. Putting all the procedures together, we have created a game of snake chess.

The Program

```
Option Base 1
Dim c (10) As Variant
Dim r (10) As Variant

Dim x As Integer
Dim m As Integer
Dim n As Integer
Dim num As Integer
Dim totalnum As Single
Dim totalnum1 As Single
```

```
Dim player As Integer
Dim t As Integer

Private Sub Command2_Click()
'To move the chess pieces to the original position
Image1 (0).Move 10200, 5520
Image1 (1).Move 10200, 6480
Totalnum = 0
totalnum1 = 0
Label2.Caption = ""
MMControl1.Command = "close"
End Sub


Private Sub Command3_Click ()
End
End Sub


Private Sub Form_Load ()
'To assign the column and row coordinates to all the boxes
c (1) = 600
r (1) = 8200
For i = 1 To 9
c (i + 1) = c (i) + 800


Next
For j = 1 To 9
r (j + 1) = r (j) — 800
Next
End Sub


'To roll the die
Private Sub roll ()
x = x + 10
Randomize Timer
num = Int(1 + Rnd * 6)
For i = 0 To 6
Shape1 (i).Visible = False
Next
If num = 1 Then
Shape1 (3).Visible = True
Shape2.FillColor = &HC0C0C0
```

```
End If
If num = 2 Then
Shape1 (2). Visible = True
Shape1 (4). Visible = True
Shape2.FillColor = &H8080FF
End If
If num = 3 Then
Shape1 (2). Visible = True
Shape1 (3). Visible = True
Shape1 (4). Visible = True
Shape2.FillColor = &H80FF&
End If
If num = 4 Then
Shape1 (0). Visible = True
Shape1 (2). Visible = True
Shape1 (4). Visible = True
Shape1 (6). Visible = True
Shape2.FillColor = &HFFFF00
End If
If num = 5 Then
Shape1 (0). Visible = True
Shape1 (2). Visible = True
Shape1 (3). Visible = True
Shape1 (4). Visible = True
Shape1 (6). Visible = True
Shape2.FillColor = &HFFFF&
End If
If num = 6 Then
Shape1 (0). Visible = True
Shape1 (1). Visible = True
Shape1 (2). Visible = True
Shape1 (4). Visible = True
Shape1 (5). Visible = True
Shape1 (6). Visible = True
Shape2.FillColor = &HFF00FF
End If
End Sub


Private Sub Command1_Click (Index As Integer)
'To identify which player is clicking the roll die command
```

```
If Index = 0 Then
player = 1
End If
If Index = 1 Then
player = 2
End If

Timer1.Enabled = True
x = 0
End Sub

Private Sub Timer1_Timer ()
If x < 100 Then
Call roll
Else
Timer1.Enabled = False

'To move player 1 according to the total score of the die
'Movement across column 1 to column 10 and row 1 to row 10

If player = 1 Then

totalnum = totalnum + num
If totalnum < 11 Then
Image1 (0).Move c (totalnum), r (1)
If totalnum = 10 Then
Image1 (0).Move c (8), r (3)
totalnum = 28
End If
End If

If totalnum > 10 And totalnum < 21 Then
Image1 (0).Move c (21 — totalnum), r (2)
If totalnum = 17 Then
Image1 (0).Move c (4), r (4)
Totalnum = 37
End If
End If
If totalnum > 20 And totalnum < 31 Then
Image1 (0).Move c (totalnum — 20), r(3)
End If
```

```
If totalnum > 30 And totalnum < 41 Then
Image1 (0).Move c (41—totalnum), r(4)
If totalnum = 34 Then
Image1 (0).Move c(5), r(2)
totalnum = 16
End If
If totalnum = 31 Then
Image1 (0).Move c (10), r (7)
totalnum = 70
End If
End If

If totalnum > 40 And totalnum < 51 Then
Image1 (0).Move c (totalnum—40), r (5)
If totalnum = 45 Then
Image1 (0).Move c (4), r (9)
totalnum = 84
End If
If totalnum = 44 Then
Image1 (0).Move c(1), r(3)
totalnum = 21
End If
End If

If totalnum > 50 And totalnum < 61 Then
Image1 (0).Move c (61—totalnum), r (6)
End If
If totalnum > 60 And totalnum < 71 Then
Image1 (0).Move c (totalnum— 60), r (7)
If totalnum = 68 Then
Image1 (0).Move c (8), r (5)
totalnum = 48
End If
End If

If totalnum > 70 And totalnum < 81 Then
Image1 (0).Move c (81—totalnum), r (8)
If totalnum = 79 Then
Image1 (0).Move c (2), r (6)
totalnum = 59
End If
```

```
If totalnum = 78 Then
Image1 (0).Move c (4), r (10)
totalnum = 97
End If
End If

If totalnum > 80 And totalnum < 91 Then
Image1 (0).Move c (totalnum — 80), r (9)
End If
If totalnum > 90 And totalnum < 101 Then
Image1 (0).Move c (101 — totalnum), r (10)
If totalnum = 95 Then
Image1 (0).Move c(8), r(8)
totalnum = 73
End If
End If

If totalnum > 100 Or totalnum = 100 Then
Image1 (0).Move c (1), r(10)
End If
End If
```

'To move player 2 according to the total score of the dice

```
If player = 2 Then
totalnum1 = totalnum1 + num
If totalnum1 < 11 Then
Image1 (1).Move c (totalnum1), r(1)
If totalnum1 = 10 Then
Image1 (1).Move c (8), r(3)
totalnum1 = 28
End If
End If
If totalnum1 > 10 And totalnum1 < 21 Then
Image1 (1).Move c (21 — totalnum1), r (2)
If totalnum1 = 17 Then
Image1 (1).Move c (4), r (4)
totalnum1 = 37
End If
End If
If totalnum1 > 20 And totalnum1 < 31 Then
```

```
Image1 (1).Move c (totalnum1 — 20), r(3)
End If
If totalnum1 > 30 And totalnum1 < 41 Then
Image1 (1).Move c (41 — totalnum1), r(4)
If totalnum1 = 34 Then
Image1 (1).Move c (5), r(2)
totalnum1 = 16
End If
If totalnum1 = 31 Then
Image1(1).Move c (10), r(7)
totalnum1 = 70
End If
End If


If totalnum1 > 40 And totalnum1 < 51 Then
Image1(1).Move c(totalnum1 — 40), r(5)
If totalnum1 = 45 Then
Image1(1).Move c(4), r(9)
totalnum1 = 84
End If
If totalnum1 = 44 Then
Image1(1).Move c(1), r(3)
totalnum1 = 21
End If
End If


If totalnum1 > 50 And totalnum1 < 61 Then
Image1 (1).Move c (61 — totalnum1), r (6)
End If
If totalnum1 > 60 And totalnum1 < 71 Then
Image1 (1).Move c (totalnum1 — 60), r (7)
If totalnum1 = 68 Then
Image1 (1).Move c (8), r(5)
totalnum1 = 48
End If
End If
If totalnum1 > 70 And totalnum1 < 81 Then
Image1 (1).Move c (81 — totalnum1), r(8)
If totalnum1 = 79 Then
Image1 (1).Move c(2), r(6)
totalnum1 = 59
```

```
End If
If totalnum1 = 78 Then
Image1 (1).Move c (4), r (10)
totalnum1 = 97
End If
End If
If totalnum1 > 80 And totalnum1 < 91 Then
Image1 (1).Move c (totalnum1 — 80), r(9)
End If
If totalnum1 > 90 And totalnum1 < 101 Then
Image1 (1).Move c (101 — totalnum1), r (10)
If totalnum1 = 95 Then
Image1 (1).Move c (8), r (8)
totalnum1 = 73
End If
End If
If totalnum1 > 100 Or totalnum1 = 100 Then
Image1 (1).Move c (1), r (10)
End If
End If


'To play the applause sound when any one player reaches 100
If (totalnum > 100 Or totalnum = 100) And totalnum1 < 100 Then
Label2.Caption = "Player 1 Wins"
MMControl1.Notify = False
MMControl1.Wait = True
MMControl1.Shareable = False
MMControl1.DeviceType = "WaveAudio"
MMControl1.FileName = "D:\Liew Folder\Visual Basic program\
audio\applause.wav"
MMControl1.Command = "Open"
MMControl1.Command = "Play"


End If
If (totalnum1 > 100 Or totalnum1 = 100) And totalnum < 100
Then
Label2.Caption = "Player 2 Wins"
MMControl1.Notify = False
MMControl1.Wait = True
MMControl1.Shareable = False
MMControl1.DeviceType = "WaveAudio"
```

```
    MMControl1.FileName = "D:\Liew Folder\Visual Basic program\
audio\applause.wav"
    MMControl1.Command = "Open"
    MMControl1.Command = "Play"
    End If
    End If
    End Sub
```

24.2 Slot Machine

This a professional-looking slot machine which resembles the real machines played in the casinos in Las Vegas! In this program, the most important part of the program is inserting three image boxes into the form and programming them so that they will display a set of three different pictures randomly when the user presses on the spin button. Therefore, it involves a randomization process. Next, a timer needs to be incorporated into the procedures so that the programs can produce animated effects. In addition, you can also insert the Microsoft Multimedia Control so that it can play sounds in synchronization with the spinning of the slot machine as well as when the player hits the jackpot.

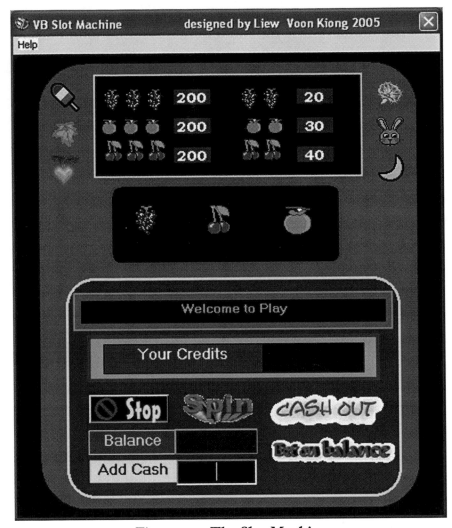

Figure 24.3 The Slot Machine

The most important part of the program is the spin procedure, which is

a = 1 + Int(Rnd * 3)
b = 1 + Int(Rnd * 3)
c = 1 + Int(Rnd * 3)

If a = 1 Then
Image1 (0).Picture = LoadPicture ("C:\Visual Basic program\ Images\grape.gif")

```
End If
If a = 2 Then
Image1(0).Picture = LoadPicture("C: \Visual Basic program\ Images\cherry.gif")
End If
If a = 3 Then
Image1(0).Picture = LoadPicture("C:\Visual Basic program\ Images\orange.gif")
End If
If b = 1 Then
Image1(1).Picture = LoadPicture("C:\Visual Basic program\Images\ grape.gif")
End If
If b = 2 Then
Image1(1).Picture = LoadPicture("C:\Visual Basic program\Images\ cherry.gif")
End If
If b = 3 Then
Image1(1).Picture = LoadPicture("C:\Visual Basic program\Images\ orange.gif")
End If

If c = 1 Then
Image1(2).Picture = LoadPicture("C:\Visual Basic program\Images\ grape.gif")
End If
If c = 2 Then
Image1(2).Picture = LoadPicture("C:\Visual Basic program\Images\ cherry.gif")
End If
If c = 3 Then
Image1(2).Picture = LoadPicture("C:\Visual Basic program\Images\ orange.gif")
End If
End Sub
```

The three random variables a, b and c will be randomly assigned the values 1, 2 and 3 through the Rnd function. Based on these three random numbers, three different pictures will be loaded into the three image boxes randomly using the LoadPicture method. Animated effects are created by putting the above procedure under the control of Timer1, which will call the spin procedure after every interval until it fulfills a certain condition. Sounds are also added using the Microsoft Multimedia Control to make the game more realistic and interesting. The amount won is controlled by the If....Then statements. For example, if two grapes appear in any two image boxes, the amount won is $20. The statements for this are:

If (a = 1 And b = 1 And c <> 1) Or (a = 1 And c = 1 And b <> 1) Or (b = 1 And c = 1 And a <> 1) Then
Label1.Caption = "You win 20 dollars"
amount = amount + 20
End If

Whenever the value of a, b or c is 1, the picture grape.gif will be loaded under the spin procedure. The above If....Then statement will check whether two grapes are loaded in any two of the three image boxes randomly; if so then the program will declare that the player has won 20 dollars. Besides that, 20 dollars will be added to the variable amount.

The Program

```
Dim x As Integer
Dim amount As Variant
Dim balance As Variant
Dim a, b, c As Integer

Private Sub Command2_Click()
End
End Sub

Private Sub betbal_Click()
Label13.Caption = Str(Val(Label6.Caption) + Val(Label13.Caption))
Label6.Caption = ""
End Sub

Private Sub Cashout_Click()
If Val(Label13.Caption) > 0 Then
balance = Val(Label6.Caption) + Val(Label13.Caption)
Label13.Caption = ""
Label6.Caption = Str(balance)
Label1.Caption = "Please bet again"
```

```
Else
Label1.Caption = "Sorry, you have no money to cash out."
End If
End Sub


Private Sub Form_Click()
Label3.Visible = False
End Sub


Private Sub Form_Load()
Label1.Caption = " Welcome to Play"
Label3.Visible = False
Image1(0).Picture  =  LoadPicture("C:\Visual  Basic  program\
Images\grape.gif")
        Image1(1).Picture = LoadPicture("C:\Visual Basic program\Images\
cherry.gif")
        Image1(2).Picture = LoadPicture("C:\Visual Basic program\Images\
orange.gif")
End Sub


Private Sub instruct_click()
Label3.Visible = True
End Sub


Private Sub Label12_Click()
Label13.Caption = Str(Val(Label13.Caption) + Val(Text2.Text))
Text2.Text = ""
End Sub


Private Sub spin_Click()
Timer1.Enabled = True
MMControl1.Command = "Close"
MMControl2.Command = "Close"
x = 0
amount = Val(Text1)
balance = Val(Label6)
End Sub


Private Sub spining_Click()
If Val(Label13.Caption) > 0 Then
Timer1.Enabled = True
```

```
MMControl1.Command = "Close"
MMControl2.Command = "close"
x = 0
amount = Val(Label13.Caption)
balance = Val(Label6)
Else
Label1.Caption = "Sorry, you have no money to spin, add cash."
End If
End Sub


Private Sub Timer1_Timer()
If x < 500 Then
spin
Else
Timer1.Enabled = False
MMControl1.Command = "Stop"
Label1.Alignment = 2
If (a = 1 And b = 1 And c <> 1) Or (a = 1 And c = 1 And b <> 1) Or (b =
1 And c = 1 And a <> 1) Then
    Label1.Caption = " You win 20 dollars"
    amount = amount + 20
End If


If (a = 2 And b = 2 And c <> 2) Or (a = 2 And c = 2 And b <> 2) Or (b =
2 And c = 2 And a <> 2) Then
    Label1.Caption = "You win 30 dollars"
    amount = amount + 30
End If


If (a = 3 And b = 3 And c <> 3) Or (a = 3 And c = 3 And b <> 3) Or (b =
3 And c = 3 And a <> 3) Then
    Label1.Caption = " You win 40 dollars"
    amount = amount + 40
End If


If (a = 1 And b = 1 And c = 1) Or (a = 2 And b = 2 And c = 2) Or (a = 3
And b = 3 And c = 3) Then


    MMControl2.Notify = False
    MMControl2.Wait = True
```

```
    MMControl2.Shareable = False
    MMControl2.DeviceType = "WaveAudio"
    MMControl2.FileName = "D:\Liew Folder\Visual Basic program\
audio\endgame.wav"
    MMControl2.Command = "Open"
    MMControl2.Command = "Play"
    Label1.Caption = "Congratulation! Jackpot!!! You win 200
dollars!"
    amount = amount + 200
    End If


    If (a = 1 And b = 2 And c = 3) Or (a = 1 And b = 3 And c = 2) Or (a = 2
And b = 1 And c = 3) Or (a = 2 And b = 3 And c = 1) Or (a = 3 And b = 2 And
c = 1) Or (a = 3 And b = 1 And c = 2) Then
    Label1.Caption = "Too bad, you lost 100 dollars"
    amount = amount—100
    End If


    If amount < 0 Then
    Label1.Caption = "Oh! You're bankrupt! Add cash to play!"
    End If
    Label13.Caption = Str(amount)
    End If
    End Sub


    Private Sub spin()
    x = x + 10
    Randomize Timer
    a = 1 + Int(Rnd * 3)
    b = 1 + Int(Rnd * 3)
    c = 1 + Int(Rnd * 3)


    MMControl1.Notify = False
    MMControl1.Wait = True
    MMControl1.Shareable = False
    MMControl1.DeviceType = "WaveAudio"
    MMControl1.FileName = "C:\Visual Basic program\audio\slot2.
wav"
    MMControl1.Command = "Open"
    MMControl1.Command = "Play"
```

```
Label1.Caption = "Good Luck!"
Label1.Alignment = a—1


If a = 1 Then
Image1(0).Picture = LoadPicture("C:\Visual Basic program\
Images\grape.gif")
End If
If a = 2 Then
Image1(0).Picture = LoadPicture("C: \Visual Basic program\
Images\cherry.gif")
End If
If a = 3 Then
Image1(0).Picture = LoadPicture("C:\Visual Basic program\
Images\orange.gif")


End If
If b = 1 Then
Image1(1).Picture = LoadPicture("C:\Visual Basic program\Images\
grape.gif")
End If
If b = 2 Then
Image1(1).Picture = LoadPicture("C:\Visual Basic program\Images\
cherry.gif")
End If
If b = 3 Then
Image1(1).Picture = LoadPicture("C:\Visual Basic program\Images\
orange.gif")
End If


If c = 1 Then
Image1(2).Picture = LoadPicture("C:\Visual Basic program\Images\
grape.gif")
End If
If c = 2 Then
Image1(2).Picture = LoadPicture("C:\Visual Basic program\Images\
cherry.gif")
End If
If c = 3 Then
Image1(2).Picture = LoadPicture("C:\Visual Basic program\Images\
orange.gif")
```

End If
End Sub

Exercise 24

1. Create a simple version of the popular monopoly game.
2. Create a slot machine that displays two rows of images.

Lesson 25

Fun and Games Programming- Part II

- Learning how to create simple games.

25.1 Boggle

This is a type of word game where players can form as many words as possible from the characters displayed on an nxn square. Words can be formed in many ways, from left to right, from right to left, top to bottom, bottom to top, diagonal, in a zigzag manner etc. as long as the letters are connected. This example is a 5x5 boggle which means it comprises 5 rows and 5 columns. Each time a player presses the shake button, a different set of characters will appear. In order to do this, I used the randomize concept. So, I created an array of characters and displayed them on an array of 25 labels. Then, I use a For...Next loop to generate the **characters**.

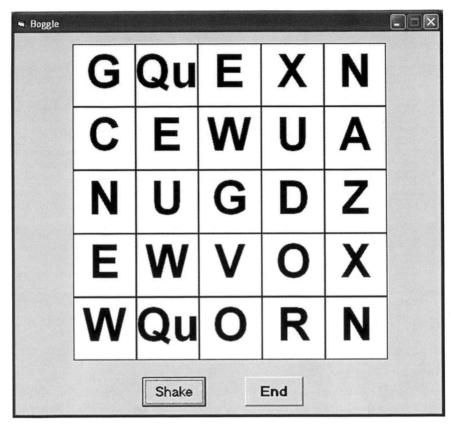

Figure 25.1

The Program

```
Dim char(26) As String
Dim I As Integer
Dim J As Integer

Private Sub Command1_Click()
char(0) = "A"
char(1) = "B"
char(2) = "C"
char(3) = "D"
char(4) = "E"
char(5) = "E"
char(6) = "G"
```

```
char(7) = "H"
char(8) = "I"
char(9) = "J"
char(10) = "K"
char(11) = "L"
char(12) = "M"
char(13) = "N"
char(14) = "O"
char(15) = "P"
char(16) = "Qu"
char(17) = "R"
char(18) = "S"
char(19) = "T"
char(20) = "U"
char(21) = "V"
char(22) = "W"
char(23) = "X"
char(24) = "Y"
char(25) = "Z"
Randomize Timer
For I = 0 To 24
J = Int((Rnd * 26))
Label1(I).Caption = char(J)
Next
End Sub
```

25.2 Reversi

This is the mini version of the typical reversi game. The interface is shown in Figure 25.2:

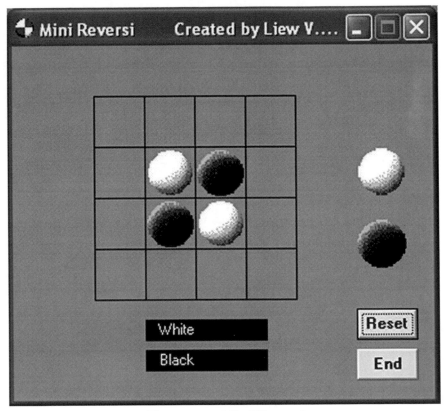

Figure 25.2 Mini Reversi

In this program, first of all I inserted an image box and then used the copy and paste method to produce a control array of 16 image boxes which represent the squares on the reversi board as shown in Figure 25.3:

Image1(12)	Image1(13)	Image1(14)	Image1(15)
Image1(8)	Image1(9)	Image1(10)	Image1(11)
Image1(4)	Image1(5)	Image1(6)	Image1(7)
Image1(0)	Image1(1)	Image1(2)	Image1(3)

Figure 25.3

Secondly, I created two sets of two dimensional arrays and declared them as Boolean, with one representing the white pieces and the other one representing the black pieces. If the white piece or the black piece occupies a square, the variable becomes true or false. Using this concept, the program can check how many white and black pieces have appeared on the board and which positions they occupy. On top of that, I inserted two images, one representing the white piece (Image 17) with its tag set as "white", and the other one representing the black piece (Image 18) with its tag set as "black". On start up, two white pieces and two black pieces are loaded in the center positions.

In order to check the status of the reversi board, i.e. to know how many white pieces and how many black pieces are currently occupying the board and which positions they are occupying, I used a sub procedure which I named as checkstatus. In this sub procedure, I used the statements

```
If Image1 (k).Picture = Image17.Picture Then
white (row, col) = True
Else
white (row, col) = False
End If
If Image1 (k).Picture = Image18.Picture Then
black (row, col) = True
Else
black (row, col) = False
End If
```

to check whether a certain image box is occupied by the white piece or the black piece. If a particular position is being occupied by the white piece, then the variable white (row, col) is declared as true or else it is declared as false. The same commands are used for the black piece. Putting the preceding statements into a nested For Loop will ensure all the positions are being checked. The positions of the reversi board can be illustrated in Figure 25.3, where (i, j) means row i and column j. The whole procedure of checkstatus is shown on the following page.

(4,1)	(4,2)	(4,3)	(4,4)
(3,1)	(3,2)	(3,3)	(3,4)
(2,1)	(2,2)	(2,3)	(2,4)
(1,1)	(1,2)	(1,3)	(1,4)

Figure 25.4

```
Private Sub checkstatus ()
k = 0
For row = 1 To 4
For col = 1 To 4
If Image1 (k).Picture = Image17.Picture Then
white (row, col) = True
Else
white (row, col) = False
End If
If Image1 (k).Picture = Image18.Picture Then
black (row, col) = True
Else
black (row, col) = False
End If
k = k + 1
Next col
Next row
```

For example, let's say we have the situation as shown in Figure 25.4, then white(1,1)=true, black(1,1)=false, white(1,2)=true, black(1,2)=false, white(1,3)=true, black(1,3)=false, white(3,2)=true, black(3,2)=false, black(2,3)=true, white(2,3)=false, black(3,3)=true, white(3,3)=false, black(4,1)=true, white(4,1)=false, black(4,4)=true and white(4,4)=false. For the blank squares, both white (i, j) and black (i, j) are false.

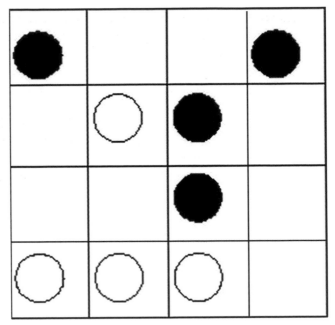

Figure 25.5

The images of the black pieces and the white pieces are loaded using the commands Image (k).Picture=Image17.Picture and Image (k). Picture=Image18.Picture.

As the reversi game involves dragging the white or black piece into a certain position, therefore a procedure is needed for the drag and drop event. To write the procedure, we need to consider a few possibilities for each and every position. For example, let's say we want to drag the white piece into square (1, 1). First of all we have to make sure that square (1, 1) is empty. Secondly we need to check that square (1, 2) is not empty or occupied by a white piece. On top of that, if square

(1, 2) is occupied by a black piece, then square (1, 3) must be occupied by a white piece for the move to be legal. Another possibility of a legal move along the first row is when square (1, 2) and square (1, 3) are occupied by black pieces while square (1, 4) is occupied by a white piece. Besides that, we also need to consider the positions along the column as well as along the diagonal. This can be figured out using the same logics.

Under the DragDrop event, I used the indices of the image1 control array to identify which position the piece is being dragged into. For example, if the index is 0, then the piece is dropped into square (1,1)

and if the index is 1 then the piece is dropped into square (1,2) and so on. In order to identify whether the white piece or the black piece is being dragged and dropped, I use the

imgtag = Source.Tag statement, where Tag is set as "white" for the white piece (Image 17) and "black" for the black piece (Image18).

In addition, I used If...Then and Select Case.... End Select commands to check whether a white or black piece can be dragged and dropped into a certain position so that the pieces trapped in between will change color. The full drag and drop procedure for position (1, 1) is shown below:

```
Private Sub Image1_DragDrop (Index As Integer, Source As
Control, X As Single, Y As Single)
imgtag = Source.Tag
checkstatus
'To check whether position(1,1) is the destination of the DragDrop
procedure and to make sure it is empty
If Index = 0 And black (1, 1) = False And white (1, 1) = False Then
Select Case imgtag
Case "white"
'Check the row positions
If black (1, 2) = True And white(1, 3) = True Then
Image1 (0).Picture = Image17.Picture
Image1 (1).Picture = Image17.Picture
End If
If black (1, 2) = True And black (1, 3) = True And white (1, 4) = True
Then
Image1 (0).Picture = Image17.Picture
Image1 (1).Picture = Image17.Picture
Image1 (2).Picture = Image17.Picture
End If
'Check the diagonal posiitons

If black(2, 2) = True And white(3, 3) = True Then
Image1(0).Picture = Image17.Picture
Image1(5).Picture = Image17.Picture
End If

If black(2, 2) = True And black(3, 3) = True And white(4, 4) = True
Then
```

```
Image1(0).Picture = Image17.Picture
Image1(5).Picture = Image17.Picture
Image1(10).Picture = Image17.Picture
End If
'Check column positions
If black(2, 1) = True And white(3, 1) = True Then
Image1(0).Picture = Image17.Picture
Image1(4).Picture = Image17.Picture
End If
If black(2, 1) = True And black(3, 1) = True And white(4, 1) = True
Then
    Image1(0).Picture = Image17.Picture
    Image1(4).Picture = Image17.Picture
    Image1(8).Picture = Image17.Picture
End If


Case "black"
If white(1, 2) = True And black(1, 3) = True Then
Image1(0).Picture = Image18.Picture
Image1(1).Picture = Image18.Picture
End If
If white(1, 2) = True And white(1, 3) = True And black(1, 4) = True
Then
    Image1(0).Picture = Image18.Picture
    Image1(1).Picture = Image18.Picture
    Image1(2).Picture = Image18.Picture
End If


If white(2, 2) = True And black(3, 3) = True Then
Image1(0).Picture = Image18.Picture
Image1(5).Picture = Image18.Picture
End If


If white(2, 2) = True And white(3, 3) = True And black(4, 4) = True
Then
    Image1(0).Picture = Image18.Picture
    Image1(5).Picture = Image18.Picture
    Image1(10).Picture = Image18.Picture
End If
'Check column
If white(2, 1) = True And black(3, 1) = True Then
```

```
Image1(0).Picture = Image17.Picture
Image1(4).Picture = Image17.Picture
End If
If white(2, 1) = True And white(3, 1) = True And black(1, 4) = True
Then
Image1(0).Picture = Image17.Picture
Image1(4).Picture = Image17.Picture
Image1(8).Picture = Image17.Picture
End If
End Select
End If
End Sub
```

For other positions, you can use similar logics. In fact, you can put everything into the above DragDrop procedure instead of writing separate procedures.

Lastly I also added the countcolor sub procedure to display the number of white and black pieces at any one time and the CheckWinner sub procedure to show who the winner is. The two sub procedures are shown below:

```
Private Sub countcolor ()
k = 0
w = 0
b = 0
For row = 1 To 4
For col = 1 To 4
If Image1 (k).Picture = Image17.Picture Then
white (row, col) = True
w = w + 1
Else
white (row, col) = False
End If
If Image1(k).Picture = Image18.Picture Then
black(row, col) = True
b = b + 1
Else
black(row, col) = False
End If
k = k + 1
Print n
```

```
Next col
Next row
Label3.Caption = Str(w)
Label4.Caption = Str(b)
End Sub

Private Sub CheckWinner ()
Call countcolor
If w + b = 16 Or b = 0 Or w = 0 Then
If w > b Then
Label5.Visible = True
Label5.Caption = "White Wins"
Else
Label5.Visible = True
Label5.Caption = "Black Wins"
End If
End If
End Sub
```

25.3 Calculator

This is a typical calculator that consists of the number buttons, the operator buttons and some additional buttons such as the memory button and the clear button.

To design the interface, you need to insert 25 command buttons, and one label that functions as the display panel. The number buttons from 1 to 9 are grouped together as a control array and named as ButtonNum while 0 is a standalone command and named as Bzero. The four basic operators are also grouped together as a control array and named as Operator. Other buttons are named appropriately according to their functions. The label is named as panel.

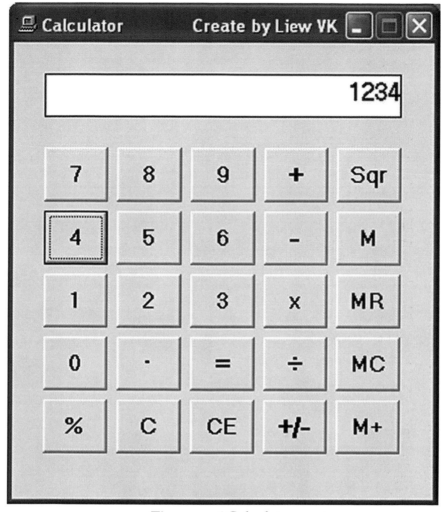

Figure 25.6 Calculator

One of the most important procedures in the program is to control the display on the panel. The procedure is

```
Private Sub ButtonNum_Click(Index As Integer)
If Num_of_digit > 0 Then
If Num_of_digit < 30 Then
panel. Caption = panel.Caption + Right$(Str(Index), 1)
Num_of_digit = Num_of_digit + 1
End If
Else
panel.Caption = Right$(Str(Index), 1)
```

```
Num_of_digit = 1
End If
CheckValue
End Sub
```

The Num_of_digit is a variable that is used to check the number of digits that appear on the display panel. The procedure will ensure that if the number of digits is more than one, the preceding digit will be pushed to the left and the succeeding digit will remain on the right. However, if the number of digits is zero, the digit clicked will just appear on the rightmost position of the panel.

Another important procedure is the procedure to perform the calculations. This can be achieved through the Operator and the Equal sub procedures. The Operator sub procedure is shown below:

```
Private Sub Operator_Click(Index As Integer)
CheckValue
If Index = 11 Then
a = displayValue
key = 1
ElseIf Index = 12 Then
b = displayValue
key = 2
ElseIf Index = 13 Then
c = displayValue
key = 3
ElseIf Index = 14 Then
d = displayValue
key = 4
ElseIf Index = 15 Then
f = displayValue
key = 5
End If
Num_of_digit = 0
newNumber = True
End Sub
```

This procedure ensures that when a particular operator button is pressed, the variable key is assigned a number so that the program knows which operator is being pressed. The calculation is then executed using the Equal sub procedure which is shown below:

```
Private Sub Equal_Click()
CheckValue
If newNumber = True Then

If key = 1 Then
e = displayValue + a
ElseIf key = 2 Then
e = b—displayValue
ElseIf key = 3 Then
e = displayValue * c
ElseIf key = 5 Then
e = (f * displayValue) / 100
ElseIf key = 4 And displayValue <> 0 Then
e = d / displayValue
Else
GoTo error
End If
If Abs(e) < 1 Then
panel.Caption = Format(e, "General Number")
Else
panel.Caption = Str(e)
End If
Else
panel.Caption = displayValue
End If
GoTo finish
error: panel.Caption = "E"
finish:
Num_of_digit = 0
newNumber = False
End Sub
```

The displayValue is the value that is displayed on the panel and this value is checked through the CheckValue sub procedure. The statements

```
If Abs(e) < 1 Then
panel.Caption = Format(e, "General Number")
Else
```

```
panel.Caption = Str(e)
End If
```

are to ensure that when the absolute value is less than 0, the zero appears in front of the decimal point, for example, 0.5 instead of just .5. The whole program is shown below:

The Program

```
Option Explicit
Dim Num_of_digit As Integer
Dim key As Integer
Dim displayValue As Variant
Dim a, b, c, d, e, f, g As Variant
Dim memo As Variant
Dim newNumber As Boolean

Private Sub BZero_Click(Index As Integer)
If Num_of_digit > 0 Then
panel.Caption = panel.Caption + "0"
Else
panel.Caption = "0"
Num_of_digit = Num_of_digit + 1
End If
CheckValue
End Sub

Sub CheckValue()
displayValue = Val(panel.Caption)
End Sub

Private Sub ButtonNum_Click(Index As Integer)
If Num_of_digit > 0 Then
If Num_of_digit < 30 Then
panel.Caption = panel.Caption + Right$(Str(Index), 1)
Num_of_digit = Num_of_digit + 1
End If
Else
panel.Caption = Right$(Str(Index), 1)
Num_of_digit = 1
End If
```

```
CheckValue
End Sub

Private Sub Clear_Click()
panel.Caption = "0"
displayValue = "0"
Num_of_digit = 0
End Sub

Private Sub ClearAll_Click()
panel.Caption = "0"
displayValue = "0"
memo = 0
End Sub
Private Sub Equal_Click()
CheckValue
If newNumber = True Then
If key = 1 Then
e = displayValue + a
ElseIf key = 2 Then
e = b — displayValue
ElseIf key = 3 Then
e = displayValue * c
ElseIf key = 5 Then
e = (f * displayValue) / 100
ElseIf key = 4 And displayValue <> 0 Then
e = d / displayValue
Else
GoTo error
End If
If Abs(e) < 1 Then
panel.Caption = Format(e, "General Number")
Else
panel.Caption = Str(e)
End If
Else
panel.Caption = displayValue
End If
GoTo finish
error: panel.Caption = "E"
finish:
```

```
Num_of_digit = 0
newNumber = False
End Sub

Private Sub MemoCancel_Click()
memo = 0
End Sub

Private Sub Memory_Click()
CheckValue
memo = displayValue
Num_of_digit = 0
End Sub

Private Sub Operator_Click(Index As Integer)
CheckValue
If Index = 11 Then
a = displayValue
key = 1
ElseIf Index = 12 Then
b = displayValue
key = 2
ElseIf Index = 13 Then
c = displayValue
key = 3
ElseIf Index = 14 Then
d = displayValue
key = 4

ElseIf Index = 15 Then
f = displayValue
key = 5
End If
Num_of_digit = 0
newNumber = True
End Sub

Private Sub Plus_minus_Click()
CheckValue
g = -1 * displayValue
displayValue = g
```

```
panel.Caption = Str(displayValue)
CheckValue
End Sub


Private Sub Poin_Click()
Static point_lock As Integer
If point_lock = 0 And Num_of_digit < 20 Then
panel.Caption = panel.Caption + "."
Num_of_digit = Num_of_digit + 1
End If
CheckValue
End Sub


Private Sub Recall_Click()
panel.Caption = Str(memo)
End Sub


Private Sub SqRoot_Click()
CheckValue
If displayValue >= 0 Then
panel.Caption = Str(Sqr(displayValue))
Else
panel.Caption = "E"
End If
Num_of_digit = 0
End Sub
Private Sub Summation_Click()
CheckValue
memo = memo + displayValue
Num_of_digit = 0
End Sub
```

Exercise 25

1. Create a calculator that can function as a normal calculator as well as a scientific calculator.
2. Create an 8x8 reversi game.

Lesson 26

Creating Educational Programs

- Learning how to create educational programs.

26.1 Kid's Math

This is a simple arithmetic educational game for children. The child who attempts the test can choose three different levels and perform three different arithmetic calculations. The performance can be evaluated by three measurements namely the total of questions attempted, the total of answers that are correct and the total score which is the percentage of right answers. The design interface is shown in Figure 26.1 and the runtime interface is shown in Figure 26.2:

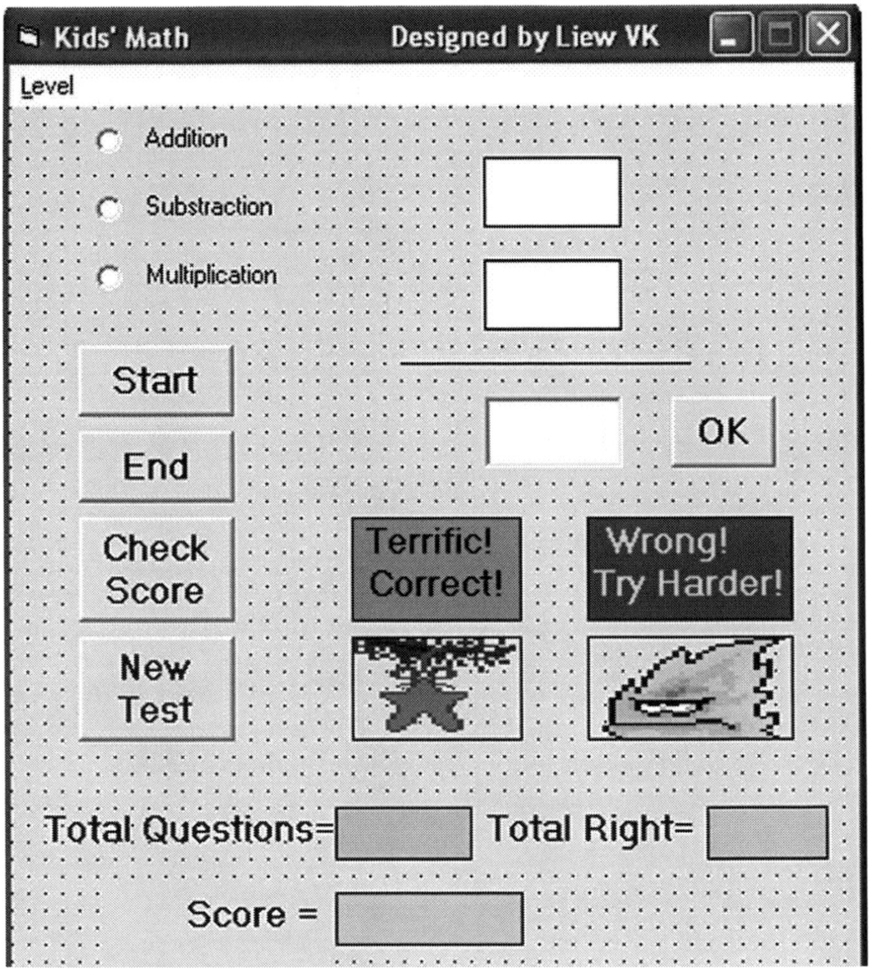

Figure 26.1 The Design Interface

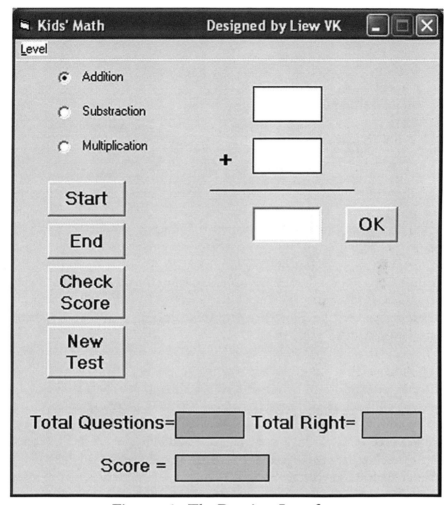

Figure 26.2 The Runtime Interface

In this program, we need to insert the following controls:
- Three option buttons
- Three text boxes
- A few labels
- Two images

The procedure to choose three different arithmetic calculations is

Private Sub Option1_Click(Index As Integer)
Select Case Index

```
Case 0
Label4.Caption = "+"
Action = "Plus"
Case 1
Label4.Caption = "-"
Action = "Minus"
Case 2
Label4.Caption = "x"
Action = "Multiply"
End Select
End Sub
```

The option buttons are grouped together as a control array and can be identified by their indices. Using the Select Case….End Select statements, the caption of Label4 which displays the operators will change according to the selection. In addition, the variable Action will be assigned different values namely "Plus", "Minus" and "Multiply". These values will be passed to the OK procedure and appropriate calculations will be performed.

A menu item "Level" for the user to choose the levels is added using the menu editor. To start the menu editor, you have to click on the tools item on the menu bar. The menu editor is shown in Figure 26.3. At the menu editor, you key in the word "Level" in the caption box and its name "level" (this can be any appropriate name) in the Name box. This is the first level menu item. To type in the second menu items, you need to click on the Next button and the right arrow key. Here you key in the words Beginner, Intermediate and Advanced. The ampersand sign '&' is used in front of all the captions (it can be in any position) so that the user can use the shortcut key to access the items. For example, to access the Level item, the user can press Alt+L.

You will notice that all the menu items will appear in the code window and you can write the event procedure for each of them. The event procedure for each of the second level menu items is very simple. It simply assigns a value to the variable n, which is n=1 for beginner, n=2 for intermediate and n=3 for advanced.

The procedure to randomize the process of displaying different numbers after each click of the command button "Start" or "Next" (the Start button changes to Next after the first Click) is shown below. The

Select Case .....End Select statements allow the generation of numbers for the three different levels.

```
Randomize Timer
Select Case n
Case 1
num1 = Int(Rnd * 10)
num2 = Int(Rnd * 10)
Case 2
num1 = Int(Rnd * 90) + 10
num2 = Int(Rnd * 90) + 10
Case 3
num1 = Int(Rnd * 900) + 100
num2 = Int(Rnd * 900) + 100
End Select
```

Menu Editor

Caption: &Level

Name: level

Index: [   ]   Shortcut: (None) ▼

HelpContextID: 0   NegotiatePosition: 0 - None ▼

☐ Checked   ☑ Enabled   ☑ Visible   ☐ WindowList

← → ↑ ↓   Next   Insert   Delete

&Level
····&Beginner
····&Intermediate
····&Advanced

OK

Cancel

Figure 26.3

There are some minor things to be considered before the actual calculation is done. First of all, for subtraction, we need to make sure that the value of the first number is more than the second number as this is arithmetic for kids. This is taken care of using the statement

Case "Minus"
If num1 > num2 Then
number1.Caption = num1
number2.Caption = num2
Else
number1.Caption = num2
number2.Caption = num1
End If

The above statements ensure that when the second number is larger than the first number, the second number will appear in the first text box and the first number will appear in the second text box. Secondly, to make sure that the multiplication is not too complicated, the second number will be restricted to values between 0 and 10. This can be achieved using the Right function as shown in the following statements:

```
Case "Multiply"
number1.Caption = num1
number2.Caption = Right(num2, 1)
```

The actual calculation is performed under the OK procedure or the KeyPress procedure so that the user has a choice to click the OK button or press the enter key to perform the calculation. The overall program is shown below:

The Program

```
Dim num1 As Integer
Dim num2 As Integer
Dim intNumber As Integer
Dim totalQ As Integer
Dim n As Integer
Dim Action As String
Dim answer As Integer
Dim done As Boolean
Dim score As Integer

Private Sub beginner_Click()
n = 1
End Sub

Private Sub Inter_Click()
n = 2
End Sub

Private Sub advance_Click()
n = 3
End Sub
```

```
Private Sub Command3_Click ()
'To calculate the score in percentage
Label10.Caption = Format ((intNumber / totalQ), "Percent")
End Sub

Private Sub Command4_Click()
total.Caption = ""
Label8.Caption = ""
intNumber = 0
totalQ = 0
Label10.Caption = ""
Command1.Caption = "Start"
End Sub

Private Sub Form_Load()
Option1(0).Value = True
Label4.Caption = "+"
Image1.Visible = False
Image2.Visible = False
Label6.Visible = False
Label5.Visible = False
End Sub

Private Sub Option1_Click(Index As Integer)
Select Case Index
Case 0
Label4.Caption = "+"
Action = "Plus"
Case 1
Label4.Caption = "-"
Action = "Minus"
Case 2
Label4.Caption = "x"
Action = "Multiply"
End Select
End Sub

Private Sub Text3_keypress(keyAscii As Integer)
Select Case Action
Case "Plus"
answer = Val(number1.Caption) + Val(number2.Caption)
```

```
Case "Minus"
answer = Val(number1.Caption)—Val(number2.Caption)
Case "Multiply"
answer = Val(number1.Caption) * Val(number2.Caption)
End Select
If (keyAscii = 13) And answer = Val(Text3.Text) Then
Image1.Visible = True
Image2.Visible = False
Label5.Visible = True
Label6.Visible = False
If done = True Then
intNumber = intNumber + 1
total.Caption = Str(intNumber)
End If
Text3.Enabled = False
ElseIf (keyAscii = 13) And answer <> Val(Text3.Text) Then
Image1.Visible = False
Image2.Visible = True
Label5.Visible = False
Label6.Visible = True
Text3.Enabled = False
End If
End Sub

Private Sub Command1_Click()
Image1.Visible = False
Image2.Visible = False
Label6.Visible = False
Label5.Visible = False
done = True

Text3.Enabled = True
Text3.Text = ""
x = x + 1
If x > 0 Then
Command1.Caption = "Next"
End If

Randomize Timer
Select Case n
Case 1
```

```
num1 = Int(Rnd * 10)
num2 = Int(Rnd * 10)
Case 2
num1 = Int(Rnd * 90) + 10
num2 = Int(Rnd * 90) + 10
Case 3
num1 = Int(Rnd * 900) + 100
num2 = Int(Rnd * 900) + 100
End Select
Select Case Action
Case "Plus"
number1.Caption = num1
number2.Caption = num2
Case "Minus"
If num1 > num2 Then
number1.Caption = num1
number2.Caption = num2
Else
number1.Caption = num2
number2.Caption = num1
End If
Case "Multiply"
number1.Caption = num1
number2.Caption = Right(num2, 1)
End Select
Text3.SetFocus
totalQ = totalQ + 1
Label8.Caption = Str(totalQ)
End Sub

Private Sub OK_Click()
Select Case Action
Case "Plus"
answer = Val(number1.Caption) + Val(number2.Caption)
Case "Minus"
answer = Val(number1.Caption) — Val(number2.Caption)
Case "Multiply"
answer = Val(number1.Caption) * Val(number2.Caption)
End Select
```

```
If Val(Text3.Text) = answer Then
Image1.Visible = True
Image2.Visible = False
Label5.Visible = True
Label6.Visible = False
If done = True Then
intNumber = intNumber + 1
total.Caption = Str(intNumber)
End If
Else
Image1.Visible = False
Image2.Visible = True
Label5.Visible = False
Label6.Visible = True
End If
Text3.Enabled = False
done = False
End Sub
```

26.2 The Memory Game

This is a typical memory game for children. The objective of the game is to reveal the pictures that are hidden under the squares. These pictures exist in pairs. When the user clicks on the square, the pictures will be revealed. If the user clicks on the squares with the same pictures successively, the squares together with the pictures will be removed. When all the squares and the pictures are removed, the background picture will show up.

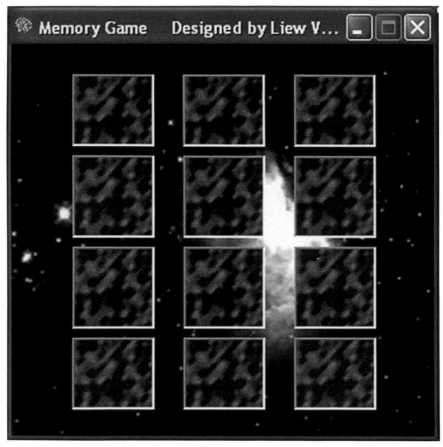

Figure 26.4

In this program, I use the images' tags to pair up the images which are hidden under the picture boxes, that is, the same images will have the same tags. The pictures and the images are both set as control arrays so that they can be manipulated using the For.....Next Loop. To check whether the images are the same or not, you can use the following procedure:

For i = 0 To 11
If Picture1(i).Visible = False Then
For j = 0 To 11
If Picture1(j).Visible = False Then
If i <> j And Image1(i).Tag = Image1(j).Tag Then
Image1(j).Visible = False
Image1(i).Visible = False
Picture1(j).Visible = False

Picture1(i).Visible = False
End If

The statement If i <> j And Image1 (i).Tag = Image1 (j).Tag checks whether the images in different positions are the same or not, and if they are the same, they will be made to disappear using the Image.Visible= False statements. A timer is used to control the program so that there is a short delay before the images disappear. The whole program is shown below:

The Program

```
Sub check()
'Check whether the images are the same or not
For i = 0 To 11
If Picture1(i).Visible = False Then
For j = 0 To 11
If Picture1(j).Visible = False Then
If i <> j And Image1(i).Tag = Image1(j).Tag Then
Image1(j).Visible = False
Image1(i).Visible = False
Picture1(j).Visible = False
Picture1(i).Visible = False
End If

If i <> j And Image1(i).Tag <> Image1(j).Tag And Image1(i).Visible =
True And Image1(j).Visible = True Then
Picture1(j).Visible = True
Picture1(i).Visible = True
End If
End If
Next j
End If
Next i

Timer1.Enabled = False
If Picture1(0).Visible = False _
And Picture1(1).Visible = False _
And Picture1(2).Visible = False _
And Picture1(3).Visible = False _
```

```
And Picture1(4).Visible = False _
And Picture1(5).Visible = False _
And Picture1(6).Visible = False _
And Picture1(7).Visible = False _
And Picture1(8).Visible = False _
And Picture1(9).Visible = False _
And Picture1(10).Visible = False _
And Picture1(11).Visible = False _
Then
MMControl1.Notify = False
MMControl1.Wait = True
MMControl1.Shareable = False
MMControl1.DeviceType = "WaveAudio"
MMControl1.FileName = "D:\Liew Folder\Visual Basic program\
audio\applause.wav"
MMControl1.Command = "Open"
MMControl1.Command = "Play"
End If
End Sub

Private Sub picture1_Click(Index As Integer)
Picture1(Index).Visible = False
Timer1.Enabled = True
End Sub
Private Sub Timer1_Timer()
check
End Sub
```

26.3 The Star War

This is a program that can demonstrate the principle of projectile in physics. At a certain angle and a certain launch velocity, the projectile can reach a certain range. The maximum range is at the angle of 45 degrees. This principle can be applied in the military field where it can simulate the launching of the missile at a certain velocity and angle in order to hit a remote target. It can also be applied in the scientific and technological fields. This game provides a good training for students in their ability to make estimations.

During the designing phase, you need to insert three images which resemble the satellites, three explosion images, the labels to display the bonus points, two text boxes for entering the values of the velocity and the angle, the image of a rocket, two timers for animation purposes and the Microsoft Multimedia Control for playing the sound of the explosion.

In this program, you can use the formulae **v sin** θ-½ **gt²** as the vertical component of the displacement and **v cos** θ as the horizontal component of the displacement (where **g** is the gravitational acceleration, **v** the launch velocity and θ the launch angle). To enable the missile to fly, you can use the combination of the **Object.Move** method and the object coordinate system, i.e. **object. left** and **object. Top**. In Visual Basic language, the procedure is

```
y = v * Sin (a * 3.141592654 / 180) * t—4.9 * (t ^ 2)
x = v * Cos (a * 3.141592654 / 180) * t
Image1.Move Image1.Left + x, Image1.Top—y
```

The above procedure will move the above missile x unit to the left and y unit to the top (or down depending on the values of y as it could be negative) after every interval until it hits the target. You can use the randomization method so that the objects will appear at different positions randomly at each new game. In addition, you can also use the randomization method to load different backgrounds at start up and at each new game.

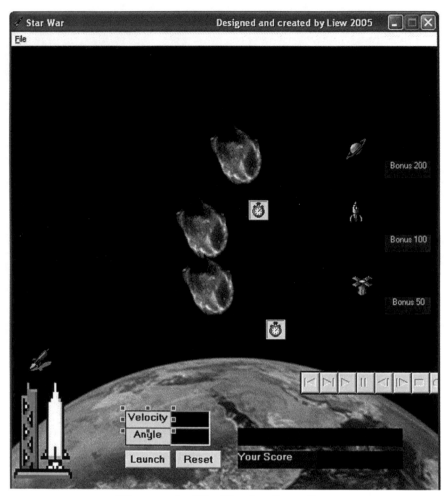

Figure 26.5 The Design Interface

The initial positions of the satellites are determined using the following procedure which ensures that they will appear within the designated window. The statements consist of the randomization process that uses the Rnd function and the use of the Left and the Top properties to determine the positions of the satellites.

```
left1 = Int(Rnd * 7000) + 1000
left2 = Int(Rnd * 7000) + 1000
left3 = Int(Rnd * 7000) + 1000
top1 = Int(Rnd * 5000) + 100
top2 = Int(Rnd * 5000) + 100
```

```
top3 = Int(Rnd * 5000) + 100
Image2.Left = left1
Image3.Left = left2
Image4.Left = left3
Image2.Top = top1
Image3.Top = top2
Image4.Top = top3
```

The procedure to show that the rocket hits the target when it moves within 240 twips right of the leftmost border of Image1(satellite) and 240 twips below the top border of Image1 (which means the rocket hits the center of Image1) is shown below.

If Image4.Visible = True And (Image1.Left < left3 + 240 And Image1.Left > left3 — 240) And (Image1.Top < top3 + 240 And Image1. Top > top3 — 240)

Timer1.Enabled = False

Call showfire

The showfire sub procedure is to start timer2 and to show the image of the explosion momentarily.

```
Private Sub Timer2_Timer()
'To delay the appearance of fire and the bonus image
w = w + 1
If w < 30 Then
Image5(i).Visible = True
Label4(i).Visible = True
Else
Image5(i).Visible = False
Label4(i).Visible = False
Timer2.Enabled = False
End If
End Sub
```

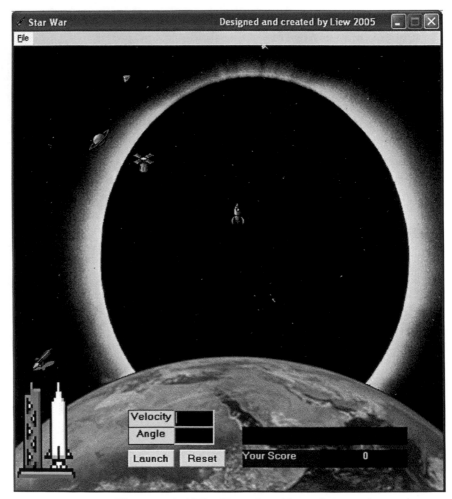

Figure 26.6 The Runtime Interface

The Program

```
Dim x As Variant
Dim a As Variant
Dim t As Variant
Dim y As Variant
Dim w As Variant
Dim i As Variant
Dim score As Integer
Dim left1, left2, left3, top1, top2, top3 As Variant
Dim backgr As Integer
```

```
Private Sub showfire()
Timer2.Enabled = True
End Sub


Private Sub Command1_Click()
Timer1.Enabled = True
End Sub


Private Sub Command2_Click()
w = 0
Image1.Visible = True
Timer1.Enabled = False
Label4(0).Visible = False
Label4(1).Visible = False
Label4(2).Visible = False
Label3.Caption = ""
Image1.Move 360, 6360
t = 0
End Sub


Private Sub Form_Click()
Label5.Visible = False
End Sub


Private Sub Form_Load()
Randomize Timer
'To choose different backgrounds at startup
backgr = Int(Rnd * 8) + 1
Select Case backgr
Case 1
Image7.Picture   =   LoadPicture("D:\Liew   Folder\Astronomy\
andromeda.jpg")
Case 2
Image7.Picture=LoadPicture("D:\Liew Folder\Astronomy\comet.
jpg")
Case 3
Image7.Picture   =   LoadPicture("D:\Liew   Folder\Astronomy\
crabnebula.jpg")
Case 4
Image7.Picture = LoadPicture("D:\Liew Folder\Astronomy\nova.
jpg")
```

```
Case 5
Image7.Picture    =    LoadPicture("D:\Liew    Folder\Astronomy\
eclipse.jpg")
Case 6
Image7.Picture = LoadPicture("D:\Liew Folder\Astronomy\horse.
jpg")
Case 7
Image7.Picture = LoadPicture("D:\Liew Folder\Astronomy\orion.
jpg")
Case Else
Image7.Picture    =    LoadPicture("D:\Liew    Folder\Astronomy\
milkyway.jpg")
End Select

'To randomly set the initial positions of the objects
left1 = Int(Rnd * 7000) + 1000
left2 = Int(Rnd * 7000) + 1000
left3 = Int(Rnd * 7000) + 1000
top1 = Int(Rnd * 5000) + 100
top2 = Int(Rnd * 5000) + 100
top3 = Int(Rnd * 5000) + 100
Image2.Left = left1
Image3.Left = left2
Image4.Left = left3
Image2.Top = top1
Image3.Top = top2
Image4.Top = top3
w = 0
score = 0
Label7.Caption = Str(score)
End Sub

Private Sub mnuExit_Click()
End
End Sub

Private Sub mnunew_Click()
w = 0
Randomize Timer
'To choose different backgrounds at startup
backgr = Int(Rnd * 8) + 1
```

```
Select Case backgr
Case 1
Image7.Picture  =  LoadPicture("D:\Liew  Folder\Astronomy\
andromeda.jpg")
Case 2
Image7.Picture = LoadPicture("D:\Liew Folder\Astronomy\comet.
jpg")
Case 3
Image7.Picture  =  LoadPicture("D:\Liew  Folder\Astronomy\
crabnebula.jpg")
Case 4
Image7.Picture = LoadPicture("D:\Liew Folder\Astronomy\nova.
jpg")
Case 5
Image7.Picture  =  LoadPicture("D:\Liew  Folder\Astronomy\
eclipse.jpg")
Case 6
Image7.Picture = LoadPicture("D:\Liew Folder\Astronomy\horse.
jpg")
Case 7
Image7.Picture = LoadPicture("D:\Liew Folder\Astronomy\orion.
jpg")
Case Else
Image7.Picture  =  LoadPicture("D:\Liew  Folder\Astronomy\
milkyway.jpg")

End Select
'To display all the objects again

left1 = Int(Rnd * 7000) + 1000
left2 = Int(Rnd * 7000) + 1000
left3 = Int(Rnd * 7000) + 1000
top1 = Int(Rnd * 5000) + 100
top2 = Int(Rnd * 5000) + 100
top3 = Int(Rnd * 5000) + 100
Image2.Left = left1
Image3.Left = left2
Image4.Left = left3
Image2.Top = top1
Image3.Top = top2
Image4.Top = top3
```

```
Image2.Visible = True
Image3.Visible = True
Image4.Visible = True
Image1.Visible = True
Timer1.Enabled = False
Label4(0).Visible = False
Label4(1).Visible = False
Label4(0).Visible = False
Label3.Caption = ""
Image1.Move 360, 6360
t = 0
End Sub


Private Sub Timer1_Timer()
MMControl1.Command = "close"
If Image1.Left < 15000 And Image1.Top < 9000 Then
v = Val(Text1.Text)
a = Val(Text2.Text)
t = t + 1
```

'To use the formulae vertical displacement=vsina- (1/2)gt ^{2} and horizontal 'displacement=vcosa*t so that it follows a parabolic trajectory

```
y = v * Sin(a * 3.141592654 / 180) * t—4.9 * (t ^ 2)
x = v * Cos(a * 3.141592654 / 180) * t
Image1.Move Image1.Left + x, Image1.Top—y
```

If Image4.Visible = True And (Image1.Left < left3 + 240 And Image1.Left > left3—240) And (Image1.Top < top3 + 240 And Image1.Top > top3—240) Then

```
    i = 2
```

'To stop the motion of the rocket and show the image of fire and bonus score

```
    Timer1.Enabled = False
    Call showfire
    Image4.Visible = False
    Image1.Visible = False
    MMControl1.Notify = False
    MMControl1.Wait = True
    MMControl1.Shareable = False
```

```
MMControl1.DeviceType = "WaveAudio"
MMControl1.FileName = "D:\Liew Folder\Visual Basic program\
audio\explosion.wav"
MMControl1.Command = "Open"
MMControl1.Command = "Play"
Label3.Caption = "You strike the satellite!"
Label4(2).Left = left3 + 240
Label4(2).Top = top3 + 240
Label4(2).Visible = True
Image5(2).Left = left3 + 240
Image5(2).Top = top3 + 240
score = score + 50
ElseIf Image3.Visible = True And (Image1.Left < left2 + 240 And
Image1.Left > left2—240) And (Image1.Top < top2 + 240 And Image1.
Top > top2—240) Then
Timer1.Enabled = False
i = 1
Call showfire
Image3.Visible = False
Image1.Visible = False
MMControl1.Notify = False
MMControl1.Wait = True
MMControl1.Shareable = False
MMControl1.DeviceType = "WaveAudio"
MMControl1.FileName = "D:\Liew Folder\Visual Basic program\
audio\explosion.wav"
MMControl1.Command = "Open"
MMControl1.Command = "Play"
Label3.Caption = "You strike the rocket!"
Label4(1).Left = left2 + 240
Label4(1).Top = top2 + 240
Label4(1).Visible = True
Image5(1).Left = left2 + 240
Image5(1).Top = top2 + 240
score = score + 100

ElseIf Image2.Visible = True And (Image1.Left < left1 + 240 And
Image1.Left > left1—240) And (Image1.Top < top1 + 240 And Image1.
Top > top1—240) Then
Timer1.Enabled = False
```

```
i = 0
Call showfire
Image2.Visible = False
Image1.Visible = False
MMControl1.Notify = False
MMControl1.Wait = True
MMControl1.Shareable = False
MMControl1.DeviceType = "WaveAudio"
MMControl1.FileName = "D:\Liew Folder\Visual Basic program\
audio\explosion.wav"
MMControl1.Command = "Open"
MMControl1.Command = "Play"
Label3.Caption = "You strike the Saturn!"
Label4(0).Left = left1 + 240
Label4(0).Top = top1 + 240
Label4(0).Visible = True
Image5(0).Left = left1 + 240
Image5(0).Top = top1 + 240
score = score + 200
End If
Else
Label3.Caption = "You miss the target!"
Timer1.Enabled = False
End If
Label7.Caption = Str(score)
End Sub


Private Sub Timer2_Timer()
'To delay the appearance of fire and the bonus image
w = w + 1
If w < 30 Then
Image5(i).Visible = True
Label4(i).Visible = True
Else
Image5(i).Visible = False
Label4(i).Visible = False
Timer2.Enabled = False
End If
End Sub
```

Exercise 26

1. Create an educational game that requires the user to add four numbers within a certain time limit.
2. Create an educational game that requires the user to identify the sound made by an animal.
3. Create a memory game that loads the hidden images randomly.
4. Create a star war program that requires the rocket to hit randomly moving targets.

Lesson 27

Working with Files

- Learning how to create a text file.
- Learning how to create a simple database management system.

27.1 Introduction

Up until Lesson 26 the programs created only accept data at runtime. When a program is terminated, the data also disappears. Is it possible to save data accepted by a Visual Basic program into a storage device, such as a hard disk or a diskette, or even a CDRW? The answer is yes. In this Lesson, we will learn how to create files by writing them into a storage device and then retrieve the data by reading the contents of the files using customized Visual Basic programs.

27.2 Creating a Text File

To create a text file, you can use the following command:
Open "fileName" For Output As #fileNumber
Each text file created must have a file name and a file number for identification. As for the file name, you must also specify the path where the file will reside.

For example:
Open "c:\My Documents\sample.txt" For Output As #1
will create a text file by the name of sample.txt in the My Document folder. The accompanying file number is 1. If you wish to create and save the file in drive A, simply change the path, as follows:
Open "A:\sample.txt" For Output As #1
If you wish to create a HTML file, simple change the extension to .html
Open "c:\My Documents\sample.html" For Output As # 2

Example 27.1 Creating a text file

```
Private Sub create_Click ()
Dim intMsg As String
Dim StudentName as String
Open "c:\My Documents\sample.txt" For Output As #1
intMsg = MsgBox ("File sample.txt opened")
StudentName = InputBox ("Enter the student Name")
Print #1, StudentName
intMsg = MsgBox ("Writing a" & StudentName & "to sample.txt
")
Close #1
intMsg = MsgBox ("File sample.txt closed")
End Sub
```

The above program will create a file sample.txt in the My Documents' folder which is ready to receive input from users. Any data input by users will be saved in this text file. Instead of print, you can also use write to save the file. After opening the file, you must always close it with the command close.

27.3 Reading a File

To read a file created in section 27.2, you can use the input # statement. The syntax is shown below:

Open "fileName" For Input As #1

You have to open the file according to its file number and the variable that holds the data. You also need to declare the variable using the DIM command.

Example 27.2 Reading a text file

```
Private Sub Reading_Click ()
Dim variable1 As String
Open "c:\My Documents\sample.txt" For Input As #1
Input #1, variable1
Text1.Text = variable1
Close #1
End Sub
```

This program will open the sample.txt file and display its contents in the Text1 textbox.

Example 27.3 A simple database management system

This is a simple database management system using a text file. First of all, the program will check whether the text file is open or not and if the file does not exist, the program prompts the user to create the file by displaying the create button. However, if the file is already there, the program will change the caption of the create button to open file. The program uses Append in the place of Output so that new data will be added to the end of the file instead of overwriting the old data. The program will also show the input box repeatedly so that the user can enter data continuously until he or she enters the word "finish".

The program also introduces the error handler to handle errors while reading the file or deleting the file because the program cannot read or delete the file when the file has not been created. The syntax for error handler is

On Error Goto Label

where the label is an error handling sub procedure. For example, when the program is trying to read the file when the file does not exist, it will go the label file_error and the error handling object 'err' will display an error message with its description property which takes the format err.description.

The program uses the vbCrLf constant when reading the data so that the data will appear line by line instead of a continuous line. The vbCrLf constant is equivalent to the pressing of the Enter key (or return key) so that the next data will go to the new line. The program is uses the Do...Loop to read all the data until it reaches the end of the file by issuing the command Loop While Not EOF(1). Below is the whole program:

```
Dim studentname As String
Dim intMsg As String

Private Sub Command1_Click()
'To read the file
Text1.Text = ""
Dim variable1 As String
On Error GoTo file_error
Open "D:\Liew Folder\sample.txt" For Input As #1
Do
```

```
Input #1, variable1
Text1.Text = Text1.Text & variable1 & vbCrLf
Loop While Not EOF(1)
Close #1
Exit Sub
file_error:
MsgBox (Err.Description)
End Sub


Private Sub Command2_Click()
'To delete the file
On Error GoTo delete_error
Kill "D:\Liew Folder\sample.txt"
Exit Sub
delete_error:
MsgBox (Err.Description)
End Sub


Private Sub create_Click()
'To create the file or open the file for new data entry
Open "D:\Liew Folder\sample.txt" For Append As #1
intMsg = MsgBox("File sample.txt opened")
Do
studentname = InputBox("Enter the student Name or type finish
to end")
If studentname = "finish" Then
Exit Do
End If
Write #1, studentname & vbCrLf
intMsg = MsgBox("Writing " & studentname & " to sample.txt ")
Loop
Close #1
intMsg = MsgBox("File sample.txt closed")
End Sub
Private Sub Form_Load()
On Error GoTo Openfile_error
Open "D:\Liew Folder\sample.txt" For Input As #1
Close #1
Exit Sub
Openfile_error:
MsgBox (Err.Description), , "Please create a new file"
```

create.Caption = "Create File"
End Sub

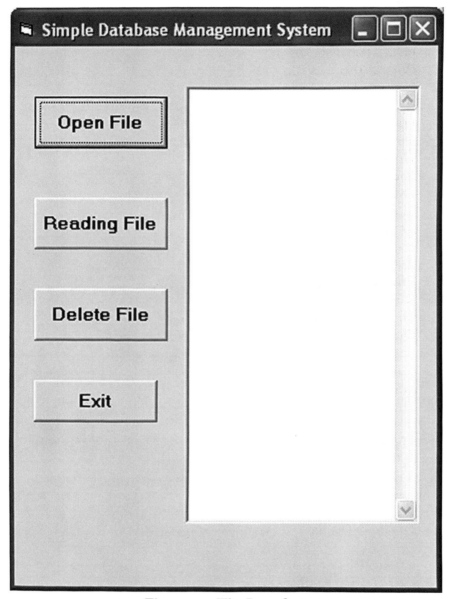

Figure 27.1 The Interface

Example 27.4
This example uses the common dialog box to create and read the

text file, which is much easier than the previous examples as many operations are handled by the common dialog box. The following is the program:

```
Dim linetext As String
Private Sub open_Click()
CommonDialog1.Filter = "Text files{*.txt)|*.txt"
CommonDialog1.ShowOpen
If CommonDialog1.FileName <> "" Then
Open CommonDialog1.FileName For Input As #1
Do
Input #1, linetext
Text1.Text = Text1.Text & linetext
Loop Until EOF(1)
End If
Close #1
End Sub
Private Sub save_Click()
CommonDialog1.Filter = "Text files{*.txt)|*.txt"
CommonDialog1.ShowSave
If CommonDialog1.FileName <> "" Then
Open CommonDialog1.FileName For Output As #1
Print #1, Text1.Text
Close #1
End If
End Sub
```

The syntax CommonDialog1.Filter = "Text files{*.txt)|*.txt" ensures that only the text file is read or saved .The statement CommonDialog1. ShowOpen is to display the open file dialog box and the statement CommonDialog1.ShowSave is to display the save file dialog box. Text1. Text = Text1.Text & linetext is to read the data and display them in the Text1 textbox. The interface is shown in Figure 27.2:

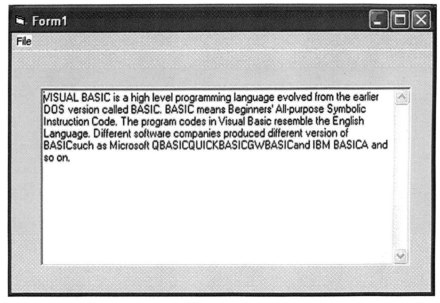

Form1

File

> VISUAL BASIC is a high level programming language evolved from the earlier DOS version called BASIC. BASIC means Beginners' All-purpose Symbolic Instruction Code. The program codes in Visual Basic resemble the English Language. Different software companies produced different version of BASICsuch as Microsoft QBASICQUICKBASICGWBASICand IBM BASICA and so on.

Figure 27.2

Exercise 27

1. Create a text file of your own using the commands you have learnt in this lesson and read the file using a text box.

2. Create a text file of your own using a common dialog box in which you can update and save the file.

Lesson 28

Creating basic database applications in Visual Basic

- Learning how to create a basic database application using data control.

Visual Basic allows us to manage databases created with different database programs such as Microsoft ® Access, Dbase, Paradox, etc. In this Lesson, we will not attempt to create database files but we will see how we can access database files in the Visual Basic environment.

Example 28.1

In this example, you will create a simple database application which enables the user to browse customers' names. To create this application, insert the data control into the new form. Place the data control somewhere at the bottom of the form. Name the data control as data_navigator. To be able to use the data control, you need to connect it to any database. You can create a database file using any database application but I suggest you use the database files that come with Visual Basic 6. Let's select NWIND.MDB as the database file. To connect the data control to this database, double-click the DatabaseName property in the properties window and select the above file. Next, double-click on the RecordSource property to select the customers' table from the database. You can also change the caption of the data control to anything but I use "Click to browse Customers" here. After that, insert a label and change its caption to Customer Name.

Finally, insert another label and name it as cus_name and leave the label empty as customers' names will appear here when the user clicks the arrows on the data control. You need to bind this label to the data control for the application to work. To do this, open the label's DataSource and select data_navigator, which will appear automatically. One more thing that you need to do is to bind the label to the correct field so that data in the field will appear on the label. To do this, open the DataField property and select ContactName. Now, press F5 and run the program. You should be able to browse all the customers' names by clicking the arrows on the data control as shown in Figure 28.1:

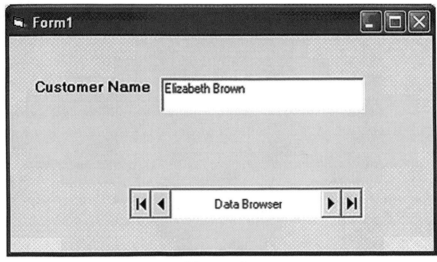

Figure 28.1

You can also add other fields using exactly the same method. For example, you can add address, city, telephone number and other information to the database browser.

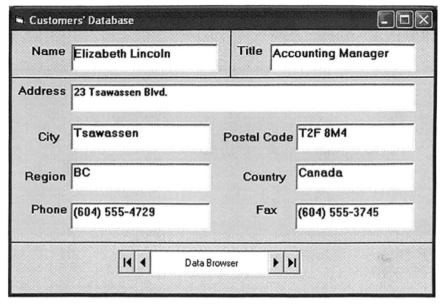

Figure 28.2

Example 28.2

Previously, you have learned how to create a simple database application using data control. In this section, you will work on the same application using slightly more advanced commands. The data control supports some methods that are useful in manipulating the database, for example, moving the pointer to a certain location. The following are some of the commands that you can use to move the pointer around.

data_navigator.RecordSet.MoveFirst

' Move to the first record

data_navigator.RecordSet.MoveLast

' Move to the last record

data_navigator.RecordSet.MoveNext

' Move to the next record

data_navigator.RecordSet.Previous

' Move to the first record

*note: data_navigator is the name of the data control

In the following example, insert four command buttons and label them as First Record, Next Record, Previous Record and Last Record. They will be used to navigate around the database without using the data control. You still need to retain the same data control (from the example in lesson 19) but set the property Visible to False so that users will not see the data control but use the buttons to browse through the database instead. Now, double-click on the command button and key in the codes according to the labels.

```
Private Sub Command1_Click ()
data_navigator.Recordset.MoveFirst
End Sub

Private Sub Command2_Click ()
data_navigator.Recordset.MoveNext
End Sub
Private Sub Command3_Click ()
data_navigator.Recordset.MovePrevious
End Sub

Private Sub Command4_Click ()
data_navigator.Recordset.MoveLast
End Sub
```

Run the application and you will obtain the interface below and you will be able to browse the database using the four command buttons.

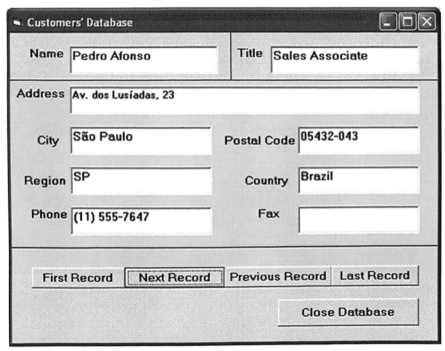

Figure 28.3

Exercise 28

1. Create a database system that can store students' information, including name, student ID, address, birthday, sex and telephone number.

Lesson 29

Creating Database Applications
Using ADO Control

- Learning how to create database applications using ADO control.

In Lesson 28, we have learned how to build Visual Basic database applications using data control. However, data control is not a very flexible tool as it works only with limited kinds of data and must work strictly in the Visual Basic environment. To overcome these limitations, we can use a much more powerful data control in Visual Basic known as ADO control. ADO stands for ActiveX data object. As ADO is ActiveX-based, it can work in different platforms (different computer systems) and different programming languages. Moreover, it can access many different kinds of data such as data displayed in Internet browsers, email text and even graphics other than the usual relational and non-relational database information. To be able to use ADO data control, you need to insert it into the toolbox. To do this, simply press Ctrl+T to open the components dialog box and select Microsoft ActiveX Data Control 6. After this, you can proceed to build your ADO-based Visual Basic database applications.

Example 29.1

This example will illustrate how to build a relatively powerful database application, a library management system, using ADO data control. First of all, name the new form as frmBookTitle and change its caption to Book Titles- ADO Application. Secondly, insert the ADO data control and name it as adoBooks and change its caption to book. Next, insert the necessary labels, text boxes and command buttons. The runtime interface of this program is shown in the diagram below; it allows adding and deleting as well as updating and browsing of data.

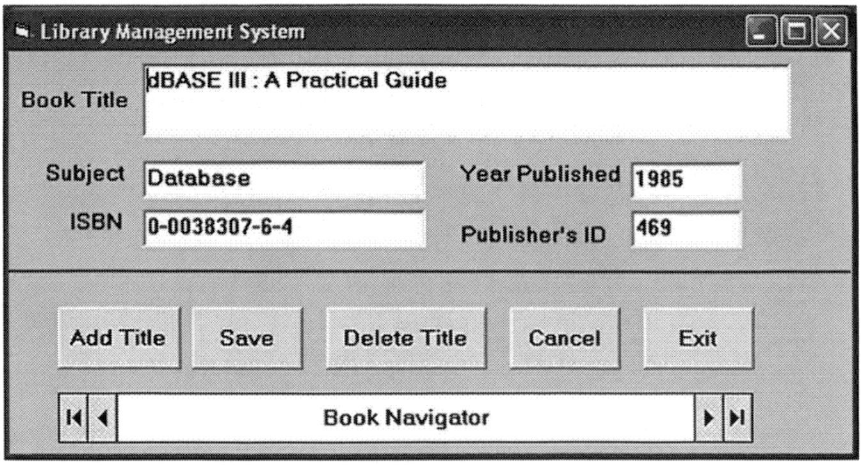

Figure 29.1 A Library Management System

The properties of all the controls are listed in Table 29.1.

Object	Property
Form	Name : FormLibrary Caption: Book Titles -Library Management System
ADO	Name :adoLibrary
Label1	Name : Titlelbl Caption: Book Title
Label2	Name: Subjectlbl Caption : Subject :Year Published:
Label3	Name: Yearlbl Caption : Year Published
Label 4	Name : ISBNlbl Caption :ISBN
Labe5	Name : PublDlbl Caption :Publisher's ID:
Text1	Name : Titletxt DataField :Title DataSource :AdoLibrary
Text3	Name: YearTxt DataField :Year Published DataSource: AdoLibrary
Text3	Name : ISBNTxt DataField :ISBN DataSource : AdoLibrary
Text4	Name: Pubtxt DataField : PublD DataSource: AdoLibrary
Text2	Name : Subject Txt DataField : Subject DataSource: AdoLibrary
Command Button1	Name :save Caption :Save
Command Button2	Name : add Caption: Add
Command Button3	Name: delete Caption: Delete
Command Button4	Name : cancel Caption :&Cancel
Command Button5	Name: exit Caption :Exit

Table 29.1

To be able to access and manage a database, you need to connect the ADO data control to a database file. We are going to use the Access database file BIBLIO.MDB that comes with Visual Basic6. To connect ADO to this database file, follow the steps below:

a) Click on the ADO control on the form and open up the properties window.

b) Click on the ConnectionString property and the following dialog box will appear.

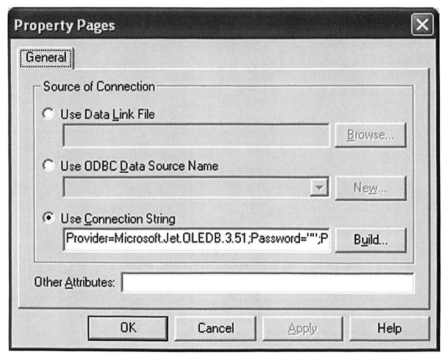

Figure 29.2

When the dialog box appears, select Use Connection String. Next, click build and at the Data Link dialog box, double-click the option labeled Microsoft Jet 3.51 OLE DB provider.

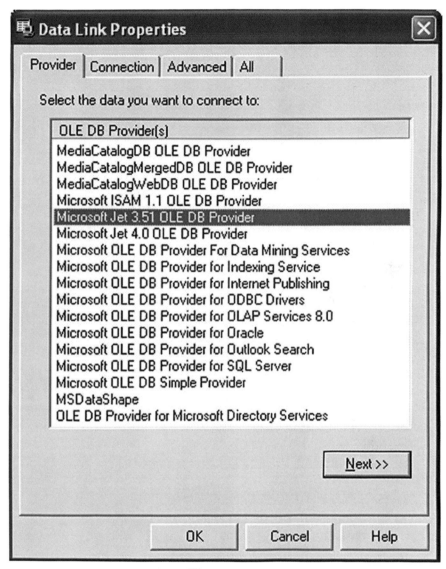

Figure 29.3

After that, click the Next button to select the file BIBLO.MDB. You can click on the Text Connection to ensure proper connection of the database file. Click OK to finish the connection. Finally, click on the RecordSource property and set the command type to adCmd Table and Table name to Titles.

Figure 29.4

Now, you need to write codes for all the command buttons, after which you can make the ADO control invisible.

For the Save button, the procedure is as follows:

```
Private Sub save_Click()
On Error GoTo errSave
AdoLibrary.Recordset.Fields("Title") = TitleTxt.Text
AdoLibrary.Recordset.Fields("Year Published") = YearTxt.Text
AdoLibrary.Recordset.Fields("ISBN") = ISBNTxt.Text
AdoLibrary.Recordset.Fields("PubID") = PubTxt.Text
AdoLibrary.Recordset.Fields("Subject") = SubjectTxt.Text
AdoLibrary.Recordset.Update
Exit Sub
errSave:
MsgBox (Err.Description)
End Sub
```

For the Add button, the procedure is as follows:

```
Private Sub Add_Click()
On Error GoTo addErr
AdoLibrary.Recordset.AddNew
Exit Sub
addErr:
MsgBox (Err.Description)
End Sub
Private Sub delete_Click()
Confirm = MsgBox("Are you sure you want to delete this record?",
vbYesNo, "Deletion Confirmation")
    If Confirm = vbYes Then
    On Error GoTo deleteErr
```

```
AdoLibrary.Recordset.delete
MsgBox "Record Deleted!",, "Message"
Else
MsgBox "Record Not Deleted!", , "Message"
End If
Exit Sub


deleteErr:
MsgBox (Err.Description), , "Empty record, please enter all the
info"


End Sub
```

For the Cancel button, the procedure is as follows:

```
Private Sub cancel_Click()
TitleTxt.Text = ""
YearTxt.Text = ""
PubTxt.Text = ""
ISBNTxt.Text = ""
SubjectTxt.Text = ""
```

Example 29.2
In the previous example, you have learned to design a database application using the ADO control. In this example, you will learn to create a more advanced database application by adding more features to the previous example. The electronic library you are going to create will be able to accept users' registrations as well as handle a login command that requires the user to enter a password, thus enhancing the security aspect of the database management system. Basically, the application will constitute a welcome menu, a registration menu, a login menu and the main database menu. The sequence of the menus is illustrated in the flowchart below:

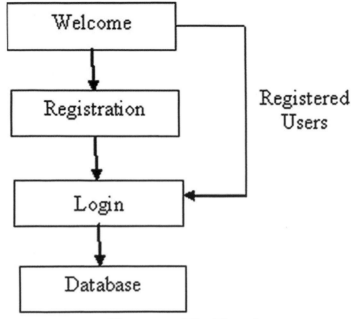

Figure 29.5 The Flowchart

In this program, you need to insert a form and design it as the Welcome menu as shown in Figure 29.6. In this form, insert three command buttons and set their properties as listed in Table 29.2.

Object	Name	Caption
Form name	main_menu	Electronic Library
command button 1	cmdRegister	Register
command button 2	cmdLogin	Login
command button 3	cmdCancel	Cancel

Table 29.2

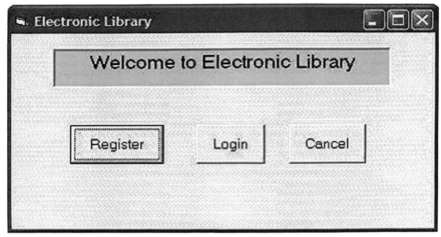

Figure 29.6 The Welcome Menu

The procedure for the welcome menu is shown below:

```
Private Sub cmdLogin_Click ()
main_menu.Hide
Login_form.Show
End Sub
Private Sub cmdRegister_Click ()
main_menu.Hide
Register. Show
End Sub
```

If a new user clicks the Register button, the registration form will appear. This registration form consists of two text boxes, three command buttons and an ADO control. Their properties are set as listed in Table 29.2 and the interface is shown in Figure 29.7. Note that the PasswordChar of the Text2 textbox is set as * which means users will not be able to see the actual characters they enter, they will only see the * symbol.

In order to connect the ADO to a database, you must create a database file in Microsoft Access. The database file must contain at least two fields, one for the user name and the other one for the password.

Object	Property
Form	Name :Register Caption: Registration Form
Text1	Name: txtName
Text2	Name: txtpassword
Text2	PasswordChar : *
command button 1	Name :cmdConfirm Caption: Confirm
command button 2	Name: cmdClear Caption: Clear
command button 3	Name: cmdCancel Caption: Cancel
ADO control name	Name :UserInfo

Table 29.3

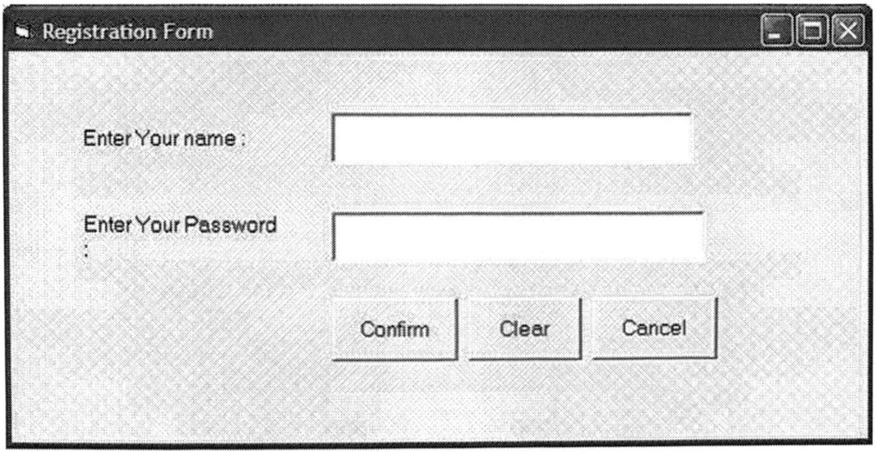

Figure 29.7 The Registration Form

The procedure for the registration form is as follows:

```
Private Sub cmdClear_Click ( )
txtName.Text = ""
txtpassword.Text = ""
End Sub
Private Sub cmdConfirm_Click ()
UserInfo.Recordset.Fields ("username") = txtName.Text
UserInfo.Recordset.Fields ("password") = txtpassword.Text
UserInfo.Recordset.Update
Register. Hide
Login_form.Show
End Sub

Private Sub Form_Load ()
UserInfo.Recordset.AddNew
End Sub
```

The login menu is illustrated in Figure 29.8:

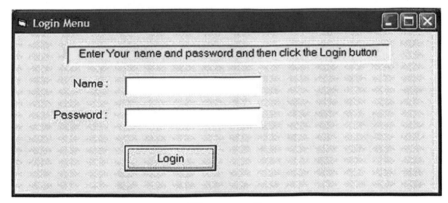

Figure 29.8

There are two text boxes and a command button. Their properties are set as follows:

Object	Property
Text1	Name: txtName
Text2	Name: txtpassword PasswordChar: *
Command button 1	Name: cmdLogin Caption: Login
Form name	Name: Login form Caption: Login Menu

Table 29.4

The procedure is as follows:

```
Private Sub cmdLogin_Click()
Dim usrname As String
Dim psword As String
Dim usernam As String
Dim pssword As String
Dim Msg As String

Register.UserInfo.Refresh
usrname = txtName.Text
psword = txtpassword.Text

Do Until Register.UserInfo.Recordset.EOF
    If   Register.UserInfo.Recordset.Fields   ("username").Value   =
usrname And Register.UserInfo.Recordset.Fields ("password").Value =
psword Then
    Login_form.Hide
    frmLibrary.Show
    Exit Sub
    Else
    Register.UserInfo.Recordset.MoveNext
    End If
    Loop
```

```
Msg = MsgBox ("Invalid password, try again!", vbOKCancel)
If (Msg = 1) Then
Login_form.Show
txtName.Text = ""
txtpassword = ""
Else
End
End If
End Sub
```

The main database interface is illustrated in Figure 29.9. Before you are able to run the program, you need to create the MS Access database file that contains a number of fields, i.e. title, author, publisher, year and category and save them as library.mdb.

After that, connect the ADO control to this database file as you have done it in the previous example. The properties of all the controls for this program are listed in Table 29.5 and the interface is shown in Example 29.5.

Object	Property
Form	Name : frmLibrary
ADO control	Name : adoLibrary
	visible : False
The Text1 textbox	Name: txtTitleA
The Text2 textbox	Name: txtAuthor
The Text3 textbox	Name: txtPublisher
The Text4 textbox	Name: txtYear
The Text5 textbox	Name: txtCategory
Command button 1	Name: cmdSave
	Caption: &Save
Command button 2	Name: cmdNew
	Caption: &New
Command button 3	Name: cmdDelete
	Caption: &Delete
Command button 4 name	Name: cmdCancel
	Caption: &Cancel
Command button 5 name	Name: cmdNext
	Caption: N&ext
Command button 6 name	Name: cmdPrevious
	Caption: &Previous
Command button 7 name	Name: cmdExit
	Caption: E&xit

Table 29.5

The procedure is as follows:
Private Sub cmdCancel_Click()
txtTitle.Text = ""
txtAuthor.Text = ""
txtPublisher.Text = ""

```vb
txtYear.Text = ""
txtCategory.Text = ""
End Sub

Private Sub cmdDelete_Click ()
Confirm = MsgBox ("Are you sure you want to delete this record?",
vbYesNo, "Deletion Confirmation")
If Confirm = vbYes Then
adoLibrary.Recordset.Delete
MsgBox "Record Deleted!", , "Message"
Else
MsgBox "Record Not Deleted!", , "Message"
End If
End Sub

Private Sub cmdNew_Click ()
adoLibrary.Recordset.AddNew
End Sub

Private Sub cmdNext_Click ()
If Not adoLibrary.Recordset.EOF Then
adoLibrary.Recordset.MoveNext
If adoLibrary.Recordset.EOF Then
adoLibrary.Recordset.MovePrevious
End If
End If
End Sub

Private Sub cmdPrevious_Click ()
If Not adoLibrary.Recordset.BOF Then
adoLibrary.Recordset.MovePrevious
If adoLibrary.Recordset.BOF Then
adoLibrary.Recordset.MoveNext
End If
End If
End Sub

Private Sub cmdSave_Click ()
adoLibrary.Recordset.Fields ("Title").Value = txtTitle.Text
adoLibrary.Recordset.Fields ("Author").Value = txtAuthor.Text
adoLibrary.Recordset.Update
```

End Sub

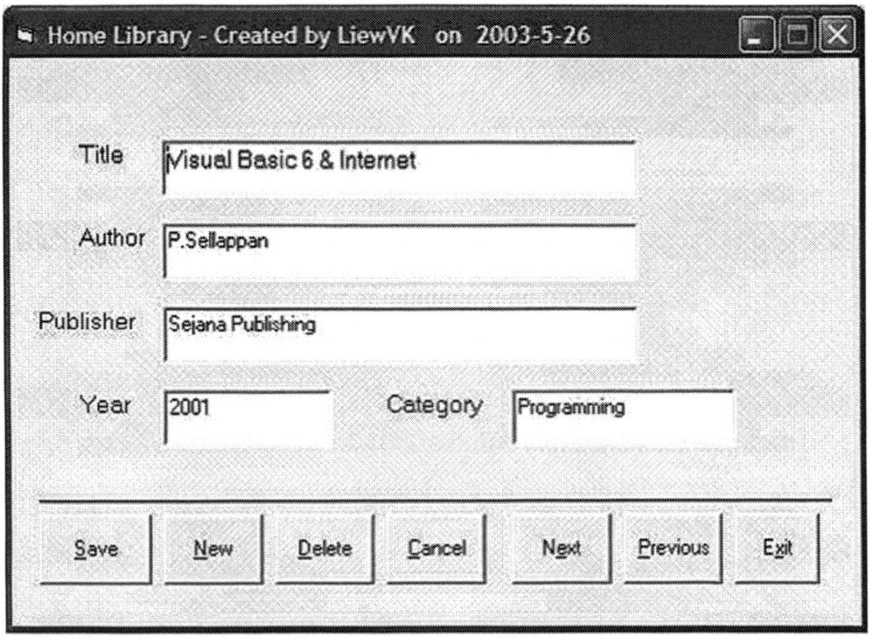

Figure 29.9 The Library System

Exercise 29

1.   Create an Inventory Management System using the ADO control. Your system should include information such as product ID, product name, cost per unit, quantity etc.

Lesson 30

Internet and Web Applications

- Learning how to create a web browser.
- Learning how to create a FTP program.

In Visual Basic, you can create Internet and web applications. For example, you can create your own customized web browser, FTP as well as an email program. All these applications are relatively easy to build.

30.1 The Web Browser

In order to create the web browser, you have to press Ctrl+T to open up the components window and select Microsoft Internet Control. After you have selected the control, you will see the control appear in the toolbox as a small globe. To insert the Microsoft Internet Control into the form, just drag the globe into the form and a white rectangle will appear in the form. You can resize this control as you wish. This control is given the default name WebBrowser1.

To design the interface, you need to insert one combo box which will be used to display the URLs. In addition, you need to insert a few images which will function as command buttons for the user to navigate the Internet: the Go command, the Back command, the Forward command, the Refresh command and the Home command. You can actually put in command buttons instead of images, but using images will definitely improve the look of the browser.

The procedures for all the commands are relatively easy to write. There are many methods, events, and properties associated with the web browser but you need to know just a few of them to come up with a functional Internet browser. They are listed in Table 30.1:

Method	Description
GoBack	To navigate backward one page in the history list.
GoForward	To navigate forward one page in the history list.
GoHome	To navigate to the default start page.
GoSearch	To navigate to the current search page.
Navigate	To navigate to the URL or to the file identified by a full path.
Refresh	To reload the file that is currently loaded.
Stop	To cancel the current web page loading operation.
Properties	
Busy	To indicate whether the web browser is engaged in navigation or downloading operations.
LocationName	To retrieve the name of the document that Internet Explorer is currently displaying.
LocationURL	To retrieve the URL of the web page that Internet Explorer is currently displaying.
Event	
DocumentComplete	Executed when a document has been completely loaded.
DownloadBegin	Executed when a navigation operation begins.
DownloadComplete	Executed when a navigation operation finishes.
FileDownload	Executed to indicate that a file download is about to occur.
NavigateComplete	Executed after navigation to a link is completed.

Table 30.1

The method navigate is to go the website specified by its Uniform Resource Locator(URL). The syntax is WebBrowser1.Navigate ("URL"). In this program, I want to load the www.vbtutor.net web page at start-up, so I type in its URL.

```
Private Sub Form_Load()
WebBrowser1.Navigate ("http://www.vbtutor.net")
End Sub
```

In order to show the URL in the combo box and also to display the page title at the form caption after the page is completely downloaded, I use the following statements:

```
Private Sub WebBrowser1_DocumentComplete (ByVal pDisp As
Object, URL As Variant)
Combo1.Text = URL
Form1.Caption = WebBrowser1.LocationName
Combo1.AddItem URL
End Sub
```

The following procedure will tell the user to wait while the page is loading.

```
Private Sub WebBrowser1_DownloadBegin ()
Combo1.Text = "Page loading, please wait"
End Sub
```

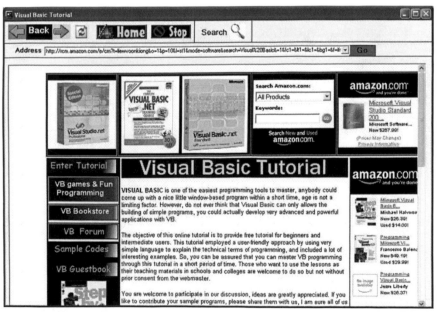

Figure 30.1 The Web Browser

The program

```
Private Sub Form_Load ()
WebBrowser1.Navigate ("http://www.vbtutor.net")
End Sub

Private Sub Image1_Click ()
WebBrowser1.GoHome
End Sub
Private Sub Image2_Click ()
On Error Resume Next
WebBrowser1.GoForward
End Sub

Private Sub Image3_Click ()
On Error Resume Next
WebBrowser1.GoBack
End Sub

Private Sub Image4_Click ()
WebBrowser1.Refresh
End Sub

Private Sub Image5_Click ()
WebBrowser1.Stop
End Sub

Private Sub Label2_Click ()
WebBrowser1.Navigate (Combo1.Text)
End Sub

Private Sub Label4_Click ()
WebBrowser1.GoSearch
End Sub

Private Sub WebBrowser1_DocumentComplete(ByVal pDisp As
Object, URL As Variant)
Combo1.Text = URL
Form1.Caption = WebBrowser1.LocationName
Combo1.AddItem URL
End Sub
```

```
Private Sub WebBrowser1_DownloadBegin()
Combo1.Text = "Page loading, please wait"
End Sub
```

30.2 The FTP program

The File Transfer Protocol is a system for transferring files between two computers over the Internet where one of the computers is normally known as the server and the other one as the client. The FTP program is very useful for website management as the webmaster can update the web pages by uploading the local files to the web server easily and normally at a much faster speed than the web browser. For normal PC users, the FTP program can also be used to download files from many FTP sites that offer a lot of useful stuff such as free software, free games, product information, applications, tools, utilities, drivers, fixes and etc.

The FTP program usually comprises an interface that shows the directories of the local computer and the remote server. Files can normally be transferred just by clicking the relevant arrows. To log into the FTP site, we normally have to key in the user name and the password; however, for public domains, we just need to type the word anonymous as the user name and you can leave out the password. The FTP host name takes the form ftp.servername.com, for example, the Microsoft FTP site's host name is ftp.microsoft.com while the Netscape FTP site is ftp.netscape.com.

The FTP program usually provides a set of commands such as ChgDir (changing directory), MkDir (Changing directory), Rename (renaming a file), view (to view a file), delete (to delete a file) etc.

If you need to use a FTP program, you can purchase one or you can download a couple of the programs that are available free of charge over the Internet. However, you can also create your very own FTP program with Visual Basic. Visual Basic allows you to build a fully functionally FTP program which may be just as good as the commercial FTP programs. The engine behind it is the **Microsoft Internet Transfer Control 6.0** in which you need to insert your form before you can create the FTP program. The name of the Microsoft Internet Transfer Control 6.0.is **Inet** and if you only put in one control, its name will be **Inet1**.

Inet1 comprises three important properties namely **Inet1.URL** which is used to identify the FTP hostname, **Inet1.UserName** which is used to accept the username and the **Inet1.Password** which is used to accept the user's passwords. The statements for the program to read the hostname of the server, the username and the password entered into the Text1 textbox, the Text2 textbox and the Text3 textbox by the user are shown below:

Inet1.URL=Text1.Text
Inet1.UserName=Text2.Text
Inet1.Passoword=Text3.Text

After the user enters the above information, the program will attempt to connect to the server using the following command, where Execute is the method and DIR is the FTP command that will read the list of files from the specified directory of the remote computer and you need to use the **getChunk** method to actually retrieve the directory's information.

Inet1.Execute, "DIR"

After connecting to the server, you can choose the file to download from the remote computer by using the statement

Inet1.Execute, , "get" & remotefile & localfile

where remotefile is the file of the remote site and localfile is the file of the local system. However, very often you need to provide the full path of the local file, which you can do by modifying the above syntax to the following syntax:

Inet1.Execute , , "get" & remotefile & localpath & remotefile

The above statements will ensure that the remote file will be downloaded to the location specified by the localpath and the file downloaded will assume the same name as the remote file. For example, the remote file is **readme.txt** and the localpath is **C:\temp** , so the downloaded file will be saved in **C:\temp\readme.txt**.

In order to monitor the status of the connection, you can use the **StateChanged** event that is associated with Inet1 together with a set of the state constants that are listed in the Table 30.2:

Constant	Value	Description
icHostResolvingHost	1	The control is looking up the IP address of the specified host computer.
icHostResolved	2	The control successfully found the IP address of the specified host computer.
icConnecting	3	The control is connecting to the host computer.
icConnected	4	The control successfully connected to the host computer.
icRequesting	5	The control is sending a request to the host computer.
icRequestSent	6	The control successfully sent the request.
icReceivingResponse	7	The control is receiving a response from the host computer.
icResponseReceived	8	The control successfully received a response from the host computer.
icDisconnecting	9	The control is disconnecting from the host computer.
icDisconnected	10	The control successfully disconnected from the host computer.
icError	11	An error occurred in communicating with the host computer.
icResponseCompleted	12	The request has been completed and all data has been received.

Table 30.2

Under the StateChanged event, you use the Select Case…End
Select statements to notify the users regarding the various states of the
connection. The procedure is shown below:

```
Private Sub Inet1_StateChanged(ByVal State As Integer)
Select Case State
Case icError
MsgBox Inet1.ResponseInfo, , "File failed to transfer"
Case icResolvingHost
Label6.Caption = "Resolving Host"
Case icHostResolved
Label6.Caption = "Host Resolved"
Case icConnecting
Label6.Caption = "Connecting Host"
Case icConnected
Label6.Caption = "Host connected"
Case icReceivingResponse
Label6.Caption = "Receiving Response"
Case icResponseReceived
Label6.Caption = "Got Response"
Case icResponseCompleted
Dim data1 As String
Dim data2 As String
MsgBox "Download Completed"
End Select
End Sub
```

The states of the connection will be displayed in Label6.

The FTP program that I have created contains a form and a dialog
box. The dialog box can be added by clicking on the Project item on the
menu bar and then selecting the Add Form item on the drop-down list.
You can either choose a normal dialog box or a login dialog box. The
function of the dialog box is to accept the FTP address, the username
and the password and then connect to the server. After a successful
login, the dialog box will be hidden and the main form will be presented
for the user to browse the remote directory and to choose certain files
to download.

The interface of the login dialog is shown in Figure 30.2:

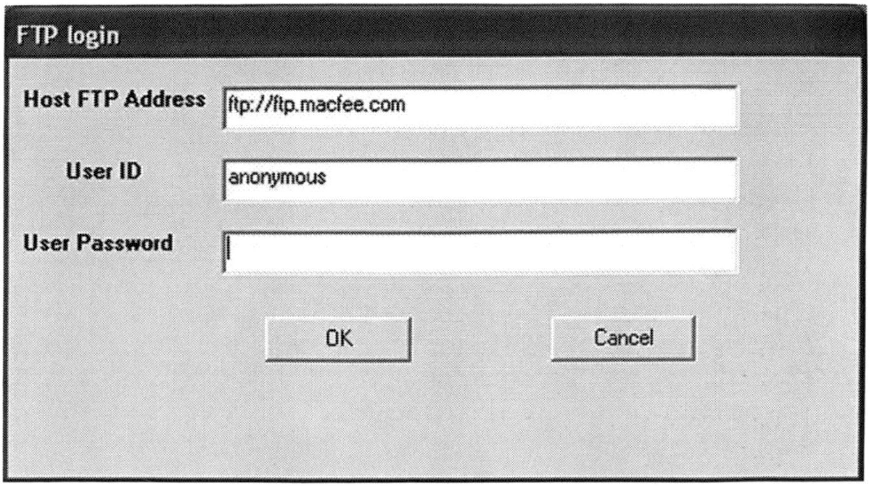

Figure 30.2 The FTP Login Form

The states of the connection will be displayed in the label at the bottom. The program for the login dialog is:

```
Option Explicit

Private Sub OKButton_Click()
Inet1.URL = Text1.Text
Inet1.UserName = Text2.Text
Inet1.Password = Text3.Text
Inet1.Execute , "DIR"
Form1.Show
Dialog.Hide
End Sub

Private Sub Inet1_StateChanged(ByVal State As Integer)
Select Case State
Case icError
MsgBox Inet1.ResponseInfo, , "File failed to transfer"
Case icResolvingHost
Label6.Caption = "Resolving Host"
Case icHostResolved
Label6.Caption = "Host Resolved"
Case icConnecting
Label6.Caption = "Connecting Host"
Case icConnected
```

```
Label6.Caption = "Host connected"
Case icReceivingResponse
Label6.Caption = "Receiving Response"
Case icResponseReceived
Label6.Caption = "Got Response"
Case icResponseCompleted
Dim data As String
Dim data1 As String

MsgBox "Transfer Completed"
Do
data1 = Inet1.GetChunk(1024, icString)
data = data & data1

Loop While Len(data1) <> 0
Form1.Text6.Text = data
End Select
End Sub
Private Sub CancelButton_Click()
Text1.Text = ""
Text2.Text = ""
Text3.Text = ""
End Sub
```

The statement data1 = Inet1.GetChunk (1024, icString) is to use the getChunk method to grab information of the remote directory and then display the files of the directory in the Text6 textbox.

After logging in, the main form will be presented as shown in Figure 30.3:

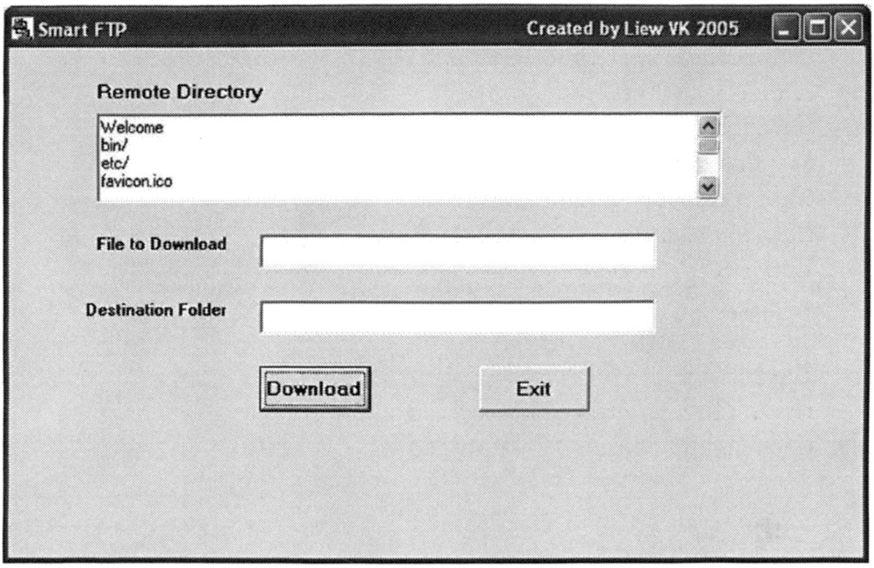

Figure 30.3

The program to download the file is:

```
Dim remotefile As String
Dim mypath As String
Dim cmd As String

Private Sub Command1_Click ()
remotefile = Text4.Text
mypath = Text5.Text
cmd = "GET " & remotefile & " " & mypath & remotefile
Inet1.Execute , cmd
End Sub

Private Sub Command2_Click()
Inet1.Cancel
End
End Sub

Private Sub Form_Load()
Dialog.Show
Form1.Hide
End Sub
```

```
Private Sub Inet1_StateChanged (ByVal State As Integer)
Select Case State
Case icError
MsgBox Inet1.ResponseInfo, , "File failed to transfer"
Case icResponseCompleted
MsgBox "Download Completed"
End Select
End Sub
```

Exercise 30

1.   Create your own customized web browser.
2.   Create your own customized FTP program.

Bibliography

'The MSDN Library'
URL: http://msdn.microsoft.com/library/

Cornel,G. 1996, *The Visual Basic 4 for Windows 95 Handbook*, Osborn McGraw-Hill, Berkeley.

Davis, H. 2003, *Visual Basic.Net for Windows*, Peachpit Press, Berkeley.

Deitel, H.M, Deitel, P.J & Nieto, T.R. 1999, *Visual Basic 6 –How to Program*, Prentice Hall, New Jersey.

Harvorson, M. 1998, *Microsof®t Visual Basic 6.0 Profesional Step by Step*, Microsoft Press.

Koay, C.W. 2000, *Microsoft Visual Basic 6.0 Step by Step*, Venton Publishing, KL.

Perry, G. 1993, *Absolute Beginner's Guide to Qbasic*, Sams Publishing, Carmel.

Sellappan, P. 2001, *Visual Basic 6 & Internet*, Sejana Publishing, PJ, Malaysia.

Made in the USA
Lexington, KY
28 February 2010